French-Beaded Flowers
New Millennium Collection

Dalene Kelly

746.5
Kel

Published by

700 East State Street • Iola, WI 54990-0001
715/445-2214 • FAX: 715/445-4087   www.krause.com

Please call or write for our free catalog of publications. Our toll-free number to place an order or obtain a free catalog is 800-258-0929, or please use our regular business telephone 715-445-2214.

All photography, including cover art, by Dalene Kelly.
All patterns designed and copyrighted by Dalene Kelly.

Library of Congress Catalog Number: 2001096272

ISBN: 0-87349-357-5

Without the constant help and support of my husband, Van,
it probably would have taken me years to complete this book.

Thank you for taking over so many of my duties.

Thank you for keeping my nose to the grindstone.

Table of Contents

Introduction

The technique is referred to as French Beading. It's commonly recognized that French and other European peasants created this art when they collected discarded glass beads and used them to create arrangements and flowered memorial wreaths. Although it's listed along with other beading techniques, French Beading is more like sculpting than sewing. The beads are first strung onto a spool of wire. The wire is then bent and twisted into the flower shapes.

Therefore, even with a pattern, the French-Bead artist has to have some knowledge of flowers. Patterns will give you a pile of parts, but it's up to you to assemble them in the right direction. What is the RIGHT direction?

The next time you receive one of those beautifully photographed seed catalogs, file it with your beading supplies. No pattern or explanation can compare to a photo or the live plant. Since most companies are trying to sell the exquisite blooms, the catalogs are excellent references for beading.

When French Beading, some patterns are quite lifelike while others are created in a manner that merely suggests reality. In most cases, large flowers are beaded to depict more detail than the smaller varieties.

As you begin accumulating a pile of flower parts, it's easy to forget exactly what you are creating. Therefore, this simple diagram of common names (fig. 1) can be used as a quick reference. If a pattern doesn't have all these parts, don't panic. This is an art, not a science. A rose is a rose.

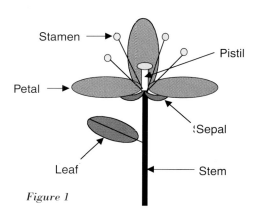

Figure 1

Typical Assembly

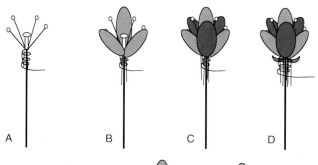

A   B   C   D

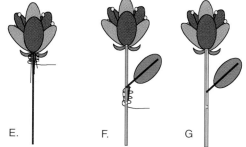

E.   F.   G

(Lightly, tape the stem wire.)

A. Use light-gauge wire to secure the pistil and stamens in place.

B. and **C.** Add the petals either one at a time or in groups. Wire them in place.

D. Position and wire the sepals in place.

E. Trim the wires to different lengths so the stem will have a smooth appearance. Tape over the exposed construction wire.

F. Position the leaf at the desired level. Wire it in place.

G. Tape over the exposed construction wire.

Figure 21

Materials, Tools, and Supplies

Beads

Finish

Begin by choosing only glass seed beads that appear uniform in size and shape. They can be found in transparent, opaque (shiny, silk, or matte), pearl (painted), and lined finishes. Although the first three are used interchangeably, lined beads can produce some special problems. The lining materials in these beads can deteriorate over a period of time. Sunshine, cleaning products, and sometimes even the act of stringing the beads can ruin the color.

Shape

Round seed beads are the beads of choice. However, particularly on very large flowers, cut seed beads can produce a very elegant effect.

Size

To reproduce the flowers in this book, choose either a size 10/0 or size 11/0. Size 10/0 is easier to work with, while size 11/0 produces a somewhat more delicate petal. All of the flowers photographed in this book are done with size 10/0.

Quantities

All of the quantities given are estimates. It's usually safest to buy extra, as some will inevitably end up escaping to the floor.

Seed beads are available either loose or strung. For ease and speed, you will probably be much happier finding a supplier that carries strung beads (mostly Czechoslovakian). If you can't find them locally, many are available on the Internet. However, loose beads can also be used easily if you invest a little more money and purchase a bead spinner (or stringer).

The quantities for the patterns in this book are based on these approximate figures:

- 16–17 beads per inch
- 18" per strand
- 12 strands per hank
- 20–24 hanks per kilo (2.2 lbs)

Wire

Finish

Wire is metal, and metal rusts. Therefore, my first choice is always a painted or coated wire. A wide range of colors, as well as gold and silver, can be found in the jewelry and bead departments of your local craft store. For a more economical source of green, black, and white, check out the paddle wire in the floral and bridal departments. I really like 30-gauge floral paddle wire for all of my assembly. It's cheap, and it won't show once the flower is taped.

Sizes

You will use a 26- or 28-gauge wire for most flower parts. The 28-gauge wire is easier to use, but 26-gauge makes a more durable flower. If you are using color-coated copper wire, switch to 24- or 26-gauge. These "craft" or "artistic" type wires are very flexible. On long spear-shaped leaves, try a 22-gauge wire for stiffness. Use 30- to 34-gauge wire for assembly and lacing. If you have trouble handling the wire, experiment with different sizes and materials. The ultimate decision on wire is up to your personal preference.

Stem wire is available in pre-cut painted lengths in the floral department. Listed here are suggested sizes:

Small flowers—18-gauge

Medium to large flowers—14- to 16-gauge

Large or un-balanced flowers (like orchid plants)—1/8" round rod stock, threaded rod stock, cut up coat hangers, or any really stiff wire or rod

Floral Tape

In the floral department, look for regular, wax-coated paper tape. When your flower is completed, smoothly wrap the entire stem with floral tape, and then rub the stem to seal the wax on the tape. This will provide a waterproof seal.

Tools

Wire cutters—Choose comfortable-to-use, sharp, hobby or jewelry front-cutters. Side-cutters are more difficult to handle.

Flat, long-nosed pliers—Excellent for stretching and straightening bent wire.

Needle-nosed pliers—Choose ones with cutters, and save your regular cutters from having to cut heavy stem wire.

Scissors—Small, sharp, and comfortable to use.

Hem gauge or ruler—The hem gauge is preferred because it can be set to the size needed, thereby insuring that all of the petals are uniform.

Darning needle—Use this to lace large leaves and petals.

Divided or flat lunch tray (optional)—Lay or glue felt inside the sections. It makes a wonderful work area, and it keeps your loose beads off the floor.

Hemostats—These are available in medical, hardware, or sporting goods (hook removers) stores. In my opinion, this is your most important tool.

Seed Bead Sizes	
7/0	4mm
8/0	3.1mm
9/0	2.7mm
10/0	**2.3mm**
11/0	**2.1mm**
12/0	1.9mm
13/0	1.7mm
14/0	1.6mm

Wire Gauges		
Gauge	Inches	mm
—	.125 (⅛)	3.2
16	.063	1.6
18	.048	1.2
20	.035	.88
22	.029	.73
24	.023	.58
26	.018	.46
28	.016	.41
30	.014	.36
32	.013	.33
34	.012	.30

General Instructions

Basic Method

1. Begin by transferring your beads onto the spool of wire. If using strung beads, hold the string taut and slide the wire through several inches at a time. If using loose beads, "spear" them onto the wire one at a time, or use a bead spinner. Put enough beads on the wire to complete the entire petal or leaf. It can be very difficult to make up for a shortage of beads. Err on the side of excess.

2. Determine (from the pattern) the size of your "basic" beaded row. Count (or measure) the required amount of seed beads; slide them toward the tip, leaving several inches of bare basic wire. Hold the beads in place by pinching the wire below them. Wrap the wire loosely around your hand, forming the "basic loop." Bring the wire up under the beads, and twist several times (fig. 2). If you have trouble keeping your basic row on the wire, try bending the tip of the wire into a tight loop before beginning. (You will now be wrapping beads up one side and down the other side of the first basic row.)

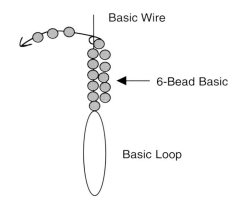

Figure 3

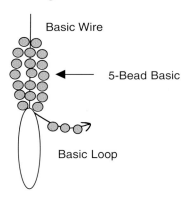

Figure 4

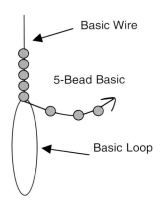

Figure 2

3. Keep your basic wire straight at all times! Push some beads forward, and bring the wire to the top of the basic row. Cross OVER then UNDER the basic wire; pull the wire tight (fig. 3). Follow the same procedure, going down the other side. Rows are counted straight across the center, so you have now completed three rows (fig. 4).

4. Proceed in the same manner, until you have the desired number of rows.

To form a rounded petal: Keep the wire very close and straight across the previous row when crossing the basic wire.

To form a pointed petal: Cross the basic wire at a 45° angle, leaving a very slight space before your over-and-under twist.

To make even more of a point: Add an extra bead to the top of your basic wire, between the rows (fig. 5). This is not mentioned in most patterns, but it can be

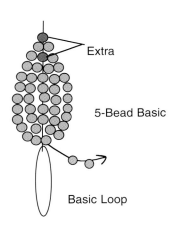

To form sharper points, add extra beads to the basic wire between rows.

Figure 5

used to accomplish the desired effect. Long, narrow, pointed leaves and petals are especially enhanced by the use of extra beads.

5. To end the flower, check the pattern to determine the number of wires you should have remaining. Use one of the methods below to cut the wire from the spool. The bulkiness of the wires during construction and the support needed for each petal will determine how you should cut the piece from the spool. The more wires you leave, the stiffer it will be.

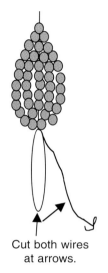

3 Wires (stiff)—Cut the basic loop open at the bottom, and pull out some spool wire. Cut the spool wire and twist the three wires (fig. 6).

Cut both wires at arrows.

Figure 6

2 Wires (medium)—Cut the spool wire 1/2" from the bottom of the piece. Cut the bottom of the basic loop open, and twist (fig. 7).

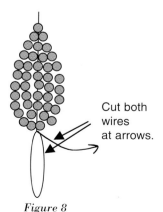

Cut both wires at arrows.

Figure 8

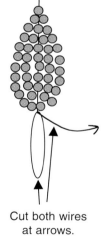

Cut both wires at arrows.

Figure 7

1 Wire (light)—Cut both the spool wire and one side of the basic loop 1/2" from the piece, and twist (fig. 8).

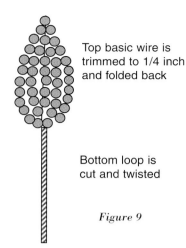

Top basic wire is trimmed to 1/4 inch and folded back

Bottom loop is cut and twisted

6. Cut the top section of the basic wire to a 1/4" length. Fold it down tightly against the back of the piece (fig. 9).

Figure 9

7. Twist the bottom wires with the hemostats. When twisting wires, grab the wire tips with the locking hemostats, hold the flower part in one hand, and put the middle finger of your other hand through one of the handle loops. Pull tight, rotating your wrist. The result is a smooth, even stem that will not fall apart later. CAUTION! Twist only until smooth and even (fig. 10). If you get carried away, you'll lose your stem!

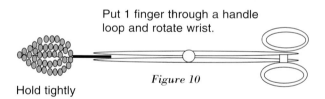

Put 1 finger through a handle loop and rotate wrist.

Figure 10

Hold tightly

8. On long or wide pieces, it's necessary to Lace the rows together in order to get a smooth and neat appearance.

Lacing

Thread a piece of 30-gauge (or finer) wire through a darning needle. Twist the needle to secure the wire, and then use one of the two methods below.

Method 1

Beginning in the center of the back of the piece, use an over-and-under motion to weave the wire to the outside edge. Then turn (running stitch), and use the same stitch to weave back across to the far edge. Turn, and weave back to the center. Pull the ends together, twist, and cut (fig. 11).

Method 2

Beginning at the edge of the back, twist the loose end of the wire around the outside row of beads. Working on the back side, use a backstitch to work across to the far edge. Twist the end around the last row again to secure and trim (fig. 11).

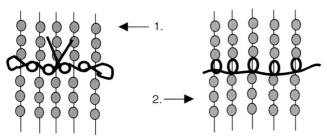

Figure 11

Stem Stiffening

Method 1

For long, slender leaves that are meant to stand up straight, incorporate an additional stem wire into the construction. After you measure your basic row of beads, hold the extra, light-gauge stem wire against the back of the beads. On each round, wrap the bead wire around both the extra and the basic wires. When the leaf is finished, trim and twist the extra wire right along with the basic wire (fig. 12).

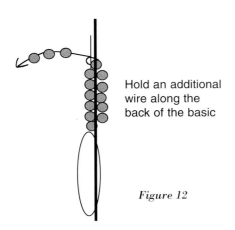

Hold an additional wire along the back of the basic

Figure 12

Method 2

For large, round leaves that just need support at the base, add only enough wire to thicken the short, twisted stem. After the leaf is completed, but before you twist the stem wire, cut a piece of wire that is twice as long as the distance from the bottom of the basic wire to the top of the lower, wrapped area.

Fold the cut piece of wire in half. From the right side of the leaf, insert one end of the folded wire, at the bottom, between rows 1 and 2. Insert the other end, at the bottom, between rows 1 and 3. Lightly twist the entire length of the cut wire. Then, combine the twisted wire with the stem wires and twist again (fig. 13).

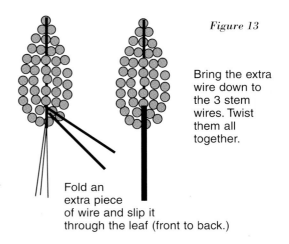

Figure 13

Bring the extra wire down to the 3 stem wires. Twist them all together.

Fold an extra piece of wire and slip it through the leaf (front to back.)

Taping

To finish the piece, tape the exposed wire with floral tape. You may also choose to bead, floss, or otherwise cover the stems. However, be sure to tape them first. It waterproofs the wire and provides a good non-skid base for anything you may choose to add.

Floral tape is usually found in 1/2" widths. Use as is or, for ease in handling when working on small pieces, remove a length of tape, cut it in half lengthwise, and use the 1/4" tape for taping small stems and leaves.

Lightly stretch the tape to activate the wax. Hold the tip against the bloom end of the wire; twirl the

Figure 14

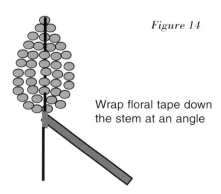

Wrap floral tape down
the stem at an angle

wire between your fingers as you move the tape downward. This will create a tight, smooth spiral. Once the entire area is covered, tear off the tape. Then pinch, smooth, and rub the stem so that the tape edges fuse together (fig. 14).

Flossing Stems

This is done just like, but over the top of, your tape. The most elegant type of floss to use is untwisted silk. Because this is somewhat expensive and hard to find, feel free to experiment with a range of different materials.

Beading Stems

This is most impressive on large flowers and branches. Make sure to tape the stem first, and then string at least five feet of beads. Do the buds and small branches first. Allowing about 2" of bare wire to trail down the stem, hold the bare end of the wire tight against the bottom of the bud. Wrap tightly twice around the stem. Slide the beads forward on the wire, and hold them tightly in place while wrapping them around and down the stem (just like taping).

I keep my other thumbnail tight against the previously wound row. Then, as I wrap the next time around, the new row actually pushes my thumbnail down the stem. When you get to a leaf, pull the leaf downward. Bead tight into the crevice. Pull the leaf back up and bead around until you meet the leaf again.

At this time, let the beads slide back, and wrap the bare wire once around the base of the leaf. Push the beads back up the wire, and continue to wrap the beads down to the point where the stems (branches) meet.

End here by wrapping the bare wire several times around the stem, as close to the beads as possible. Then spiral the bare wire down a few inches before cutting. Do the same thing to the rest of the small stems and branches. Then, after wiring the branches together, proceed in the same manner to do the large flower stems.

Here are two tips to help the process along: 1) If you have enough room, start your wrapping by putting the first row of beads between the petals and the sepals. Wrap the bare wire around each sepal, just as you did the leaf on the bud stem. 2) DON'T cut the wire when you reach the joints. Wrap the bare wire once around each joint and continue downward. Stop at least 1" to 3" from the bottom. End as before. Cut the wire, and cover all exposed ends with floral tape.

Other Commonly Used Techniques

Continuous Loops

Without a basic wire, form a loop of beads in the desired length, cross the wires, and give one full twist. Beginning at the base of the loop just completed, repeat the process for the desired number of loops (fig. 15).

Figure 15

Use at least 1 full twist at the bottom of each loop. (Always twist all of the loops in the same direction.)

Continuous Double Loops

Use the same technique as the Continuous Loops to form the first loop. Then wrap the beads around the outside of the loops a second time. Twist and move on to the next loop (fig. 16).

Figure 16

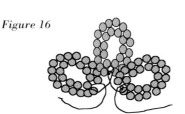

When you apply the second row of beads around the outside of the first, wrap the wire around the bottom. Do not try to twist again.

Continuous Crossover Loops

Beginning with the Continuous Loop technique, make the loop, twist to secure, and then bead up the front of the loop and down the back. Twist, and move on to the next loop. This makes a 4-row crossover loop. For the 3-row crossover, bead up the front and leave bare wire down the back. Twist and move on to the next loop (fig. 17).

Figure 17

3

Row

4

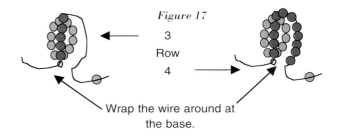

Wrap the wire around at the base.

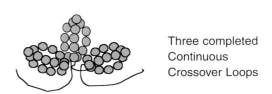

Three completed Continuous Crossover Loops

Beehive (Cup)

This technique is accomplished by bending the basic wire, the basic loop, or both, backwards, at a set angle, while continuing to add rows. A slight bend of both wires will form a type of raised-button shape, similar to the center of a daisy. A sharp bend of one wire will create a tapered cup (snapdragon petal). A sharp bend of both basics will create a thimble shape (coneflower center). See illustration for side views (fig. 19).

Weaving or Basket Bottom

This technique looks just as it sounds. However, you don't actually weave over and under the wires. Instead, every time you come to one of the spread wires (spokes), you wrap the wire around it, as if it were the basic wire.

Cut a determined number of wires. Hold them together in a bundle, and wrap the bare end of the beaded wire twice, tightly around the centers. Spread the wires open, like the spokes of a wheel, and bead around the center. (Some patterns will tell you how many beads to put between the spokes, others will not.) These are counted as rounds, instead of rows (fig. 20).

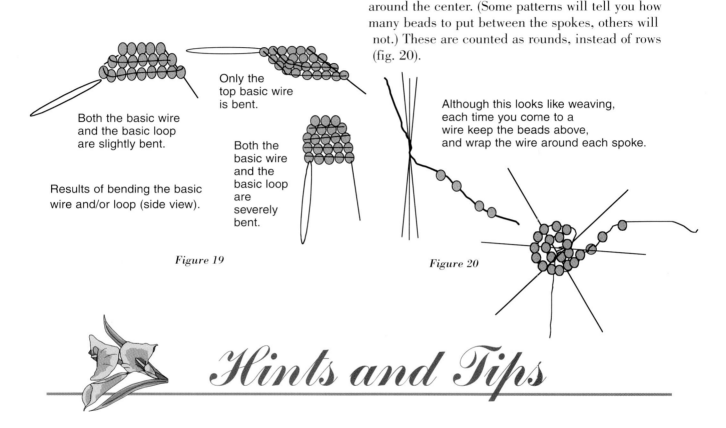

Both the basic wire and the basic loop are slightly bent.

Results of bending the basic wire and/or loop (side view).

Only the top basic wire is bent.

Both the basic wire and the basic loop are severely bent.

Figure 19

Although this looks like weaving, each time you come to a wire keep the beads above, and wrap the wire around each spoke.

Figure 20

Hints and Tips

How many beads should I string at a time?

If you're making multiple petals with the same color beads, be sure to string enough to complete at least the part you are making. Always err on the side of too many. If you do run short, over estimate the amount of wire you will need, cut it from the spool, and add the beads onto the cut end.

Never try to attach a second wire in the middle of a petal. It may look fine when you're finished, but you will have lost the overall integrity of the piece. Strange and unusual twists are bound to appear in years to come. Personally, I like to get most of my stringing done at the beginning, so I can continue moving from petal to petal without interruption.

What is a bead spinner, and why should I use one?

Many bead stores, craft shops, and Internet craft sites carry a nifty little item called a bead spinner (or stringer). It's a small wooden or plastic bowl with a center shaft. When you spin the shaft, the beads are forced out against the sides in a whirling mass. Although a curved needle is usually supplied with the spinner, a French Beader can go one better on the concept. All you have to do is bend the tip of your beading wire into a hook and lower it into the spinning beads. The beads will literally jump onto the wire. This not only allows you to easily use loose beads, but it's also an absolute blessing when mixing colors for variegated leaves and petals. If you intend to do a lot of beading, a bead spinner is worth its weight in gold!

How should I clean my French-Beaded flowers?

If you are not sure whether or not the beads have a lined or dyed finish applied to them, the safest way to clean your flowers is to simply run them under hot water. If you are sure that they are "color safe," a mild spray cleaner can also be used. The most important thing is to make sure that they are dried thoroughly! On hot sunny days, set them in the sun for an hour or two. On cool days, place them in the oven on the COOLEST setting for several hours, or use a hair dryer to blow them dry.

What kind of container should I use to display my flowers?

French-Beaded flowers are very heavy! Everyone who lifts one for the first time is amazed by the weight. This can create some unique problems when trying to assemble a bouquet. In other words, don't place a bouquet in Grandma's antique, bone china vase and walk away. It will, most likely, come crashing down.

Make sure that you choose containers that are extremely stable and have rather broad, flat bottoms. It's often necessary to have enough room to also add some material to the vase for added weight. A display that continually crashes to the floor is not only nerve wracking, but it usually ends up all bent and twisted.

How do I add extra weight to my vase?

There are many ways to add extra weight to a favorite vase or container. One way is to fill your containers with marbles, stones, or BBs. Although rather messy, floral clay can also add enough extra weight to hold the flowers. If the bouquet is to stay in the vase "forever," floral clay can even be melted (gently) and poured in after the bouquet is complete. In most cases, floral foam will NOT work. The flowers are just too top heavy to remain secure in Styrofoam®.

If all else fails, make your own pot. Tape over the drainage hole, and fill a clay pot with wet plaster of Paris. Leave enough empty room at the top to later add camouflage. Lightly wrap a piece of paper around a flower stem several times, and tape it. Push it all the way down into the pot. Then, pull out the stem, leaving the paper behind. Once the plaster becomes firm, twist the paper and pull it out. If some remains, use tweezers or hemostats to reach in and pull it out.

Using the same plaster method, you can cut lengths of plastic drinking straws, tape the ends, and insert them into the plaster. Add a couple extra to each pot, for future use. Once the plaster hardens, cut the straws off even with the surface. Disguise the plaster by covering its surface with moss or shredded bark.

Can I add scent to my French-Beaded flowers?

To give your flowers that extra touch of reality, scented oils can be added to the pot. However, NEVER put scented oils on your beads! The ingredients can discolor the beads!

How do I keep the dogs and kids from knocking over my projects?

Check out second-hand sources for a small computer cart on wheels. Not only will you have several shelves for your supplies, but the keyboard shelf is just the right size for your beading tray.

Long-stemmed Sweetheart Rose

This is my most often requested ready-made flower. Nature provides us with every shade of white, pink, orange, lavender, and bi-color bloom. However, for a great contemporary look, try making these with black petals and either clear or metallic leaves. The result is quite dramatic! This time, I chose the patriotic look.

Materials Needed

1 hank of petal-color beads
1/2 hank of green beads
26-gauge beading wire
30- to 34-gauge assembly wire
18" of 14- or 16-gauge stem wire
1/2" green floral tape

Petals (round top, round bottom)
> **Make 5 (petal color)**
> 8-bead basic, 3 rows (Reduce to 1 wire.)
> **Make 5 (petal color)**
> 4-bead basic, 7 rows (Reduce to 1 wire.)
> **Make 5 (petal color)**
> 4-bead basic, 9 rows (Reduce to 1 wire.)
> **Make 5 (petal color)**
> 5-bead basic, 11 rows (Reduce to 1 wire.)
> **Make 5 (petal color)**
> 5-bead basic, 13 rows (Reduce to 1 wire.)

Sepals (pointed top, round bottom)
> **Make 5 (green)**
> 3-bead basic, 7 rows (Reduce to 1 wire.)

Leaves (pointed top, round bottom)
> **Group #1**
> **Make 1 (green)**
> 8-bead basic, 11 rows (Leave 3 wires, and twist.)
> **Make 2 (green)**
> 8-bead basic, 7 rows (Leave 3 wires, and twist.)
> **Group #2**
> **Make 1 (green)**
> 8-bead basic, 13 rows (Leave 3 wires, and twist.)
> **Make 2 (green)**
> 8-bead basic, 9 rows (Leave 3 wires, and twist.)

Assembly

1. Lightly tape the stem wire.

2. Starting with the smallest petals, hold a single petal so that the base is even with the top of the stem wire. Using the thin assembly wire, tightly wrap the petal in place (2-3 passes). One at a time, position each petal around the stem and secure in the same manner.

3. When all five petals are added, go on to the next size, and repeat the procedure. Make sure to place each row tightly against the previous row. Failure to do so will leave unsightly gaps in your bloom.

4. When all 25 petals have been added, arrange the sepals in the same manner. Secure the sepals, and cut the assembly wire.

5. Turn the rose upside down, pull the wires slightly away from the stem, and cut them all to the same length, 1/2" from the bloom.

6. Tape the entire stem again, making sure to wrap the assembly area with several layers, thereby producing the rose-hip effect.

7. Leaf Group Assembly:

Group #1

a. After twisting the wires, cut a length of floral tape in half (lengthwise). Beginning at the base of the beads, tape about halfway down each leaf.

b. With the largest leaf at the top and the two small ones opposite each other (fig. 23), hold the leaves together, and twist the wires together.

c. Tape the twisted area, and slightly flatten the lower half. This will lessen any bulges on the flower stem.

d. Position this group several inches below the bloom, and tape it in place.

Group #2

Assemble as above, and place this group several inches below and opposite Group #1.

Figure 23

Cymbidium Orchid

For many years, my youngest brother brought me an Easter corsage. I would wear it for a day and then mourn its demise. Last year I decided to immortalize it. Now I can remember the sentiment all year long. Thanks Darrell.

Materials Needed

2 1/2 hanks of petal-color beads

1/2 hank of contrasting-color beads

2 strands of yellow (matte) beads

1 hank of green beads

1/2 hank of brown beads (optional for beading the stem)

26-gauge beading wire

30- to 34-gauge wire (for lacing and assembly)

Two 18" pieces of 18-gauge green stem wires, cut in half (to stiffen leaves)

14" of 1/8" rod stock, or very heavy stem wire

1/2" green floral tape

1/2" brown floral tape

Petals

Make 15 (petal color) (pointed top, round bottom)

1 3/4" basic, 13 rows

    a. Add an extra bead to the basic wire on each row after row 5.

    b. Leave 3 wires, and twist.

Make 3 (contrasting color) (round top, round bottom)

1 3/4" basic, 7 rows (Leave 3 wires, and twist.)

Make 3 (Mix equal parts of petal-color and contrasting-color beads on the wire, about 1 1/2 strands of each color per petal.) (pointed top, round bottom)

1-bead basic, 23 rows

    a. Use 6 beads each for rows 1 and 2. Push them down against the basic bead, and then bead around this until you reach a total of 7 rows.

    b. On each additional row, add an extra bead to the basic wire until the petal is completed.

    c. Leave 3 wires, and twist.

Pistil

Make 3 (yellow)

    a. String 6" of beads, make a loop, and twist twice.

    b. Pinch the loop closed, twist beads (3"), and fold in half (1 1/2").

    c. Put one basic stem wire through the tip of the loop.

    d. Finish by twisting the wires.

Bud (pointed top, round bottom)

Make 2 (1 green, 1 petal color)

1 1/2" basic, 11 rows (Leave 3 wires, and twist.)

Leaves (pointed top, round bottom)

Make 4 (green)

6" basic, 9 rows

    a. After measuring the basic wire, use Stem Stiffening Method 1 to reinforce the leaf.

    b. Leave 3 wires, and twist.

Assembly

1. Lace all petals across the center.

2. Lace the leaves twice, 2" from the top and 2" from the bottom.

3. Working with the large, multicolored petal, bring the sides up to form a cone at the base of the petal. Use lacing wire to tack the sides together, about 1" from the base.

4. Slip the pistil into the cone. Hold the bases even, and twist the wires together several times. Bend the tip of the cone down slightly.

5. Position the contrasting-color petal (back side down) directly over the top of the cone. Using assembly wire, wrap the stem several times. Bend the petal into a gentle curve toward the cone.

6. Add 5 (contrasting-color) petals, one at a time, securing each with the same assembly wire. Tape with green floral tape. Assemble the other two blooms in the same manner.

7. Place the 2 buds with their back sides together. Twist the petals to form a bi-colored spiral. Twist the wires together, and tape with green floral tape. Tape the remainder of the plant in brown floral tape.

8. Allowing about 1 1/2" of green to show, wire the bud to the top of the stem. Now add each of the blooms in the same manner, leaving about 2" between them. Continue spiral wrapping the wire down to within 3" of the bottom.

9. Add two leaves, opposite each other, and wire in place. Add the last 2 leaves directly below the first 2, and finish by taping the entire stem again.

10. Hold the stem firmly. Put a distinct bend in the stem where each bud and bloom connects to the stem.

11. Optional: If you choose to bead the stems, use green for the individual bloom stems and brown for the main stem.

Large Moth Orchid

Every time another orchid blooms, I'm haunted by the fact that the flowers will soon fade away. French beading is my solution. Out come the beads, and another flower is captured.

Materials Needed

3 hanks of petal-color beads
3 hanks of green beads
1 strand of yellow beads
26-gauge beading wire
30- to 34-gauge wire (for lacing and assembly)
18" of 1/8" rod stock, or very heavy stem wire
1/2" green floral tape
1/2" brown floral tape

Centers (pointed top, round bottom)

Make 3 (petal color)

3-bead basic, 9 rows, and 2 loops

    a. After completing row 5, add 4 beads to the basic wire.

    b. Each time you cross the "extra beads," pinch the tip to form a point.

    c. Once the rows are complete, leave 5" of bare wire, and cut the wire from the spool.

    d. Add 18 yellow beads, and form two 9-bead loops at the base of the petal.

    e. Fold the loops towards the back of the petal (fig. 24).

    f. Leave 3 wires, and twist.

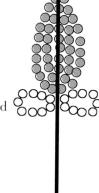

Figure 24

Make 6 (petal color)

1-bead basic, 7 rows

    a. After completing row 3, add 3 beads to the basic wire.

    b. Each time you cross the "extra beads," pinch the tip to form a point.

    c. Leave 3 wires, and twist.

Petals

Make 6 (petal color) (pointed top, round bottom)

1-bead basic, 23 rows

    a. Use 9 beads each for rows 2 and 3 (fig. 25).

    b. After completing row 9, add one bead to the basic wire for the next 4 rows.

Flatten the long rows down against the short basic.

Figure 25

c. Each time you cross the "extra bead," pinch the tip to form a point.

d. Leave 3 wires, and twist.

Make 3 (petal color) (pointed top, round bottom)

20-bead basic, 13 rows (Leave 3 wires, and twist.)

Make 6 (petal color) (round top, round bottom)

16-bead basic, 11 rows (Leave 3 wires, and twist.)

Pistils

Make 3 (petal color)

a. Leave 3" of bare wire. Use 1" of beads for the first loop and then complete the Double Crossover Loop.

b. Leave 3" of bare wire, cut, and twist.

c. Twist beaded loops.

Buds (pointed top, round bottom)

Make 1 (petal color)

12-bead basic, 13 rows (Leave 3 wires, and twist.)

Make 1 (green)

12-bead basic, 11 rows (Leave 3 wires, and twist.)

Make 2 (green)

10-bead basic, 9 rows (Leave 3 wires, and twist.)

Leaves (round top, round bottom)

Make 3 (green)

2" basic, 19 rows

a. Leave 3 wires.

b. Use Stem Stiffening Method 2 to stiffen.

Make 3 (green)

2 1/2" basic, 21 rows

a. Leave 3 wires.

b. Use Stem Stiffening Method 2 to stiffen.

Make 3 (green)

3" basic, 23 rows

a. Leave 3 wires.

b. Use Stem Stiffening Method 2 to stiffen.

Assembly

1. Lace the 9 leaves and the 6 large petals.

2. *Large Bud*

a. Hold the petal-color bud and the largest green bud back-to-back. Twist the beads into a spiral.

b. Twist the wires, and tape with green floral tape.

3. *Small Bud*

a. Hold the 2 small, green buds together, and twist into a spiral.

b. Twist the wires, and tape with green tape.

4. *Centers*

a. Cup 3 of the center pieces (1 large with loops and 2 small) backwards.

b. Hold them together with all cups facing inward. Place the large one at the bottom, a small one at each side, and add a pistil at the top.

c. Twist all the wires together. Do the same for the other 2 sets.

5. Using assembly wire, attach two large petals on either side of the center assembly.

6. Add 2 small petals to the bottom and 1 medium petal to the top.

7. Secure all the parts with assembly wire. Tightly twist all the wires together. Tape the bloom stem with green tape. Assemble the other two blooms in the same way.

8. Using brown tape, lightly tape the 1/8" rod.

9. Position the small bud at the very tip, and wire it in place.

10. About 1 1/2" from the beads, bend the stem of the large bud at a 90° angle. Wire this about 1 1/2 to 2" from the small bud. Bend the green stems of the blooms, and attach them in the same manner, alternating them on opposite sides. You should have 2 blooms on one side; there should be 1 bloom and 1 large bud on the other side. Spiral the assembly wire down the rod.

11. About 3" from the bottom of the stem, attach the 3 small leaves at the same level. Next, directly below the first group, add the 3 medium leaves, then the 3 large leaves. Secure with wire and tape.

12. Bend the rod into a gentle arc, and make sure all of the blooms are right side up.

napdragon

The reason for making this design was simple. I couldn't find a pattern for a snapdragon any- where. The more of these you add, the more fabulous your bouquet becomes.

Materials Needed

1 1/2 hanks of petal-color beads
1 1/2 hanks of green beads
26-gauge beading wire
30-gauge assembly wire
18" of 18-gauge stem wire
1/2" green floral tape

Petals (round top, round bottom)

Make 18 small cups (petal color)

1-bead basic, 13 rows

    a. After completing row 3, bend the top basic wire back to about an 80° angle. As you continue beading, you will be making a slanted cup.

    b. After you trim and twist the wires, lightly pinch the cup near the twisted wire, while tugging the other side outward. You should end up with a Beehive shape similar to Little Bo-Peep's bonnet (fig. 19, page 14).

    c. Reduce to 1 wire.

Make 18 large cups (petal color)

3-bead basic, 9 rows

    a. Bend the basic wire back to an 80° angle after row 3.

    b. Reduce to 1 wire.

Buds (Pinch loops together, and twist wires.)

Make 6 (petal color)

Leaving 2" of bare wire at the beginning and end, make two 12-bead Continuous Loops.

Make 6 (petal color)

Leaving 2" of bare wire at the beginning and end, make three 16-bead Continuous Loops.

Make 1 (green)

Leaving 2" of bare wire at the beginning and end, make five 16-bead Continuous Loops.

Sepals

Make 30 (green)

Leaving 2" of bare wire at the beginning and end, make five 12-bead Continuous Loops.

Leaves (pointed top, round bottom)

Make 15 (green)

2" basic, 5 rows (Leave 3 wires, and twist.)

Assembly

1. To make the blooms, hold a single small-cup petal and a single large-cup petal together with front sides facing. Make sure the bases are even. Twist twice to hold them together. Position a sepal (Continuous Loop) assembly at the base, with the open side facing down (under the large cup). Twist all the wires together. Trim wires to 2" and tape.

2. Position a petal-color bud in each of the remaining sepals. Twist the wires together, and tape.

3. Lightly tape the large stem wire.

4. Position the green bud tightly against the tip of the large stem wire, and wire in place. Keep the wire connected. Wire down 1", and secure 3 small buds at equal distances around the stem.

5. Tape down 1". Attach the next 3 small buds in the same manner, making sure that they are positioned below the empty spaces of the previous row.

6. Tape down 1". Attach the large buds, all of the blooms, and all of the leaves in the same manner (1" between rows, 3 per row, all spaced under the empty spaces of the row above). Tape the entire stem.

Hanging Fuchsia

Use your imagination. Make these in white, pink and white, pink and purple, or red and blue. It really doesn't matter whether you stay with one color or mix them up. They are just adorable!

Materials Needed

1 1/2 hanks of petal-color beads (If you use 2 colors, the ratio of petal to contrasting color is 50/50.)

1 1/2 hanks of light green beads

26-gauge beading wire (Colored is best for the pistil and stamens.)

30-gauge assembly wire

Three 18" pieces of 18-gauge stem wire

1/2" green floral tape

1/2" colored floral tape or silk floss to match the large petals (optional)

Cup Petals (round top, round bottom)
    Make 8 (petal or contrasting color)
4-bead basic, 5 rows (Reduce to 1 wire.)
    Make 10 (petal or contrasting color)
3-bead basic, 7 rows (Reduce to 1 wire.)
    Make 12 (petal or contrasting color)
2-bead basic, 9 rows (Reduce to 1 wire.)

Outer Petals (pointed top, round bottom)
    Make 8 (petal color)
3/4" basic, 9 rows (Reduce to 1 wire.)

Buds (pointed top, round bottom) (DON'T cut top basic wire.)
    Make 3 (petal color)
3-bead basic, 5 rows (Reduce to 1 wire.)
    Make 3 (petal color)
4-bead basic, 7 rows (Reduce to 1 wire.)

Leaves (pointed top, round bottom)
    Make 2 (green) (seed pods)
1/2" basic, 5 rows (Leave 3 wires, twist, and tape.)
    Make 2 (green)
3/4" basic, 7 rows (Leave 3 wires, twist, and tape.)
    Make 6 (green)
1" basic, 9 rows (Leave 3 wires, twist and tape.)

Pistil and Stamens
    Make 7 (petal color)
        a. Cut 4" of bead wire.
        b. Add 1 bead to the center.
        c. Fold in half, and twist the entire length.
    Make 1 (petal color)
        a. Cut 5" of bead wire.
        b. Add 3 beads to the center.
        c. Fold in half, and twist the entire length.

Assembly

1. Lightly tape the 3 stem wires.

2. Using assembly wire, attach the pistil and 7 stamens about 1/2" from the bottom of one of the stem wires. (This flower is upside down.)

3. One at a time, and still using assembly wire, attach 4 small petals with the wrong sides facing the stamens. Keeping each row tight against the previous one, add 5 medium petals and then 6 large round petals in exactly the same manner.

4. Next, with the wrong side facing out, add 4 large pointed petals. Wrap tightly. About 1/2" above the last petals, trim all the wires to the same length. Tape and bead over the 1/2" of wires. Or, using colored or white tape, tape the bundle of wires and tape 1" up the stem. (If you were not able to obtain tape to match the petals, tightly wrap the bundle with untwisted silk floss.) Using green tape, make a neat line around the top of the bundle, and cover the rest of the colored tape. Set this aside, and repeat the procedure to assemble the next blossom.

5. Using the 3 small bud petals, hold the tips together, and twist the top basic wires. Cut the top basic twist to 1/2", and bend it down between the petals. Cup the petals. Bring the bottoms together, twist, and tape. Create the large bud in the same manner.

6. Using the smallest green leaves (seed pods), twist the beads into a spiral, and tape the stems.

7. On the bottom of the last 18" of stem wire, use assembly wire to attach the 2 buds and the 2 smaller green leaves (the buds hanging down, leaves facing up). Tape over the assembly wire, and tape up the stem.

8. Hold all three large stems together. Position them so that the buds are 3" below the first flower and the second flower is 1" above the first.

9. Move up 3", add 2 leaves (facing up), and wire all the stems together.

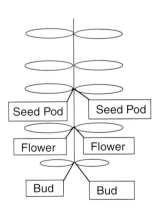

Figure 26

10. Wire up 3", and add 2 leaves and the 2 seedpods. Wire them in place. Wire up another 3". Position the last 2 leaves, and wire the rest of the stem. Tape over the entire stem (fig. 26).

11. Cup all of the small petals toward the stamens, and bend the large petals upwards.

Aztec Lily

*W*hen I first saw a photo of this unusual flower, I was entranced by the dramatic petal arrangement. This is an excellent choice for the contemporary home. It's also an impressive choice for the beginner.

Materials Needed

1 hank of red beads
1 hank of green beads
1 strand of yellow beads
26-gauge beading wire
30- to 34-gauge wire (for lacing and assembly)
18" of 16-gauge stem wire (or heavier)
1/2" green floral tape

Petals (pointed tops, round bottoms)
Make 4 (red)
2" basic, 11 rows (Leave 3 wires, and twist.)
Make 2 (red)
2 1/2" basic, 7 rows (Leave 3 wires, and twist.)

Stamens
Make 6 (yellow and red) (Use unpainted craft or beading wire.)
a. Using yellow, make two 10-bead Continuous Loops.
b. Measure 6" of spool wire, and cut. Cut the short end of the wire to 1/2".
c. Put 2" of red beads on the 6" wire.
d. Hold the short wire tight against the long wire, and push the beads up over both. Make sure the beads are tight against the bottom of the loops.
e. Shape the loops so that the stamen forms a "T."
f. Add 1" of yellow beads, and set aside.
g. Make the other 5 stamens. Next, make the pistil.

Pistil
Make 1 (yellow and red)
a. Using red beads, make three 8-bead Continuous Loops.
b. Cut the spool wire to 6".
c. Cut the short wire to 1/2".
d. In the same manner as the stamens, add 2" of red beads and 1" of yellow beads to the wire.
e. Bend the loops down against the stalk to form a knob on the end of the pistil.

Leaves (pointed top, round bottom)
Make 12 (green)
6" basic, 3 rows (Leave 3 wires, and twist.)

Assembly

1. Lace all leaves and petals.

2. Lightly tape the 18" stem wire.

3. Hold all the stamens and the pistil together in a bunch. Twist the bare wires until the beads are tight.

4. Twist the 1" of yellow beads into a spiral, leaving the red portion loose. Wrap a single strand of assembly wire around the group, placing it where the red and yellow beads meet. Twist tightly, trim to 1/4", and tuck the end into the spiral.

5. Stack 3 of the large petals (facing up), and twist the wires together. Slide the petals into a fan shape. Using a finger, hold down the center of the middle petal, and squeeze the petal into a trough. Put the stamen-pistil assembly in this trough, match the bases, and twist the wires. Curl the petals back.

6. Stack the 3 remaining petals with the large one in the center. Twist the wires. Slide the petals into a fan shape. Using assembly wire, attach the 2 petal groups to the end of the stem wire. Use the photo to determine proper petal placement.

7. Holding 3 green leaves together, twist the wires. Repeat with the rest, so that you have 4 groups of 3 leaves each. Six inches from the bottom of the stem wire, position the 4 groups of leaves around the stem, and wire them in place. Tape the entire stem.

8. Bend the large stem wire down until the blossom hangs in a drooping position.

Dutchman's Breeches

Although this flower is very easy to construct, it adds a definite point of interest to your bouquet.

Materials Needed

1 hank of white beads
3 strands of light green beads
1 strand of yellow beads
26-gauge beading wire
30-gauge assembly wire
18" 16-gauge stem wire
1/2" green floral tape

Petals (round bottom, pointed top)

Make 22 (white)
6-bead basic, 9 rows (Reduce to 2 wires, and twist.)

Stamens

Make 11 (yellow)
a. Leave 3" of bare wire. Make three 1/2" Continuous Loops.
b. Leave 3" of wire, and cut.

Leaves

Make 1 (green)
a. Leave 1" of bare wire. Make one 16-bead loop.

b. Thread the 1" of bare wire through the loop, and pull it tight. Thread it through again, and trim the short wire close to the loop.
c. Push 4 beads up tight against the loop.
d. Make 2 more 16-bead loops. Push forward another 4 beads. Repeat until you have completed a total of 17 loops with 4-bead spacers between the pairs of loops.
e. Leave 2 beads on the wire, measure 3" of bare wire, and cut.

Make 2 (green)
   Make these in exactly the same manner. However, in step d., make a total of 15 loops.

Assembly

1. Lightly tape the 18" stem wire.

2. Put two petals together, front sides facing, and lightly twist the wires. Open the petals to a flat ("T") position. Where they are joined, insert a 3-loop stamen through the petals, so that one bare wire goes between the first two beaded rows of each petal. Twist the stamen wire once or twice tight against the back of the petals. Hold all the petal and stamen wires together, twist tightly, and tape.

3. Hold a thin, flat object (such as a wooden ruler) with the edge against the center back of a petal. Fold both sides of the petal back sharply, and pinch them. Repeat the procedure on the second petal. Bend both petals backwards toward the stem.

4. Open the sepal loops so that 1 loop is back against each petal and the center one points straight outward. Repeat until you have completed all 11 blossoms.

5. Using assembly wire, attach one blossom to the tip of the stem wire. Place the next blossom at a distance, so that its sepal fits right into the V-shape of the previous one, and wire it in place. Continue until all blossoms have been wired to the stem.

6. Lightly arch the stem wire. Pull the blossoms out and down to alternate sides of the wire.

7. Stack the 3 leaves with the bases together. Twist the wires, and tape. Fan the pieces slightly so they still have the appearance of a single leaf. Pinch the uppermost loops flat. Bend them towards the tip to create a tapered effect. Tape this assembly 1" below the lowest blossom.

8. If you feel that your bouquet needs more greenery at its base, make and add more leaves. Tape them at the same level as the first.

Common Flax

The branching nature of this small-blossomed plant adds depth and symmetry to any arrangement.

Materials Needed

1/2 hank of light blue beads
5 strands of medium green beads
1 strand of yellow beads
26-gauge beading wire
26-gauge gold beading wire
12" of 16-gauge stem wire
1/2" green floral tape

Flowers
Make 9 (blue)
    a. Leave 4" of bare wire. Make five 3-row 1" Continuous Crossover Loops.
    b. Leave 4" of bare wire, and cut. Don't twist or tape.

Buds
Make 3 (blue)
    a. Leave 4" of bare wire. Make two 8-bead Continuous Loops.
    b. Measure 4" of wire, and cut.
Make 3 (blue)
    a. Leave 4" of bare wire. Make two 12-bead Continuous Loops.
    b. Measure 4" of wire, and cut.
Make 3 (blue)
    a. Leave 4" of bare wire. Make two 16-bead Continuous Loops.
    b. Measure 4" of wire, and cut.

Stamens
Make 9 (yellow beads on gold beading wire)
    a. Measure 4" of bare wire. Make five 1/2" Continuous Loops of wire containing 1 bead per loop.
    b. Measure 4" of wire, and cut.
    c. Holding the bead at the top of the loop, twist each loop into a tight stalk.

Sepals
Make 9 (green)
    a. Leave 4" of bare wire. Make four 8-bead Continuous Loops.
    b. Measure 4" of wire, and cut.

Leaves
Make 18 (green)
    a. Leave 1" bare wire. Measure 1" of beads.
    b. Make a single loop. Twist, but don't tape.
    c. Pinch the loop closed.
Make 9 (green)
    a. Leave 1" bare wire. Measure 1 1/2" of beads.
    b. Make a single loop. Twist, but don't tape.
    c. Pinch the loop closed.
Make 12 (green)
    a. Leave 1" bare wire. Measure 2" of beads.
    b. Make a single loop. Twist, but don't tape.
    c. Pinch loop closed.

Assembly

1. Lightly tape the stem wire.

2. Put a stamen group in the center of each flower. Pull the wires down tight. Twist all 4 wires (stamen and flower) together. Cut a length of floral tape to 1/4" wide. Beginning at the blossom, tape down 1". Add a small leaf, and tape down 1". Add a medium-sized leaf. Tape down 1". Set aside.

3. Cup a sepal assembly around each of the 9 buds. Pull the pieces tight against each other. Twist all 4 wires (bud and sepal) together. Tape down 1". Add a small leaf, and tape down 2".

4. Hold 1 bud and 1 flower together. Twist the bare portion of the wires, and tape down 1/2". Repeat with the remaining pieces (9 units).

5. Hold 3 units together. Twist the bare portion of the wires, and tape down 1/2". Add 2 large leaves, and tape down 1/2". Repeat twice more for 3 large units.

6. Tape one large unit to the top of the stem wire. Tape down 1", and add the second. Tape down 1", and add the third. Tape down the rest of the stem, adding large leaves at 1/2" intervals. Bend the large and small stems until most of the blossoms are at approximately the same level and the branch has a lifelike appearance.

*L*arge *O*x-eye *D*aisy, *B*lack-eyed *S*usan & *C*oneflower

These flowers are so similar that you can use the same pattern, with just a few variations, to make a multicolor bouquet.

Materials Needed

6 strands of white beads (yellow for Black-Eyed Susan, pink for Coneflower)

1 strand of yellow beads (brown for Black-Eyed Susan and Coneflower)

6 strands of green beads

26-gauge beading wire

30-gauge assembly wire

16" of 16-gauge stem wire

1/2" green floral tape

Petals
Make 1 (white)
a. Leave 3" of bare wire. Using 4" of beads per loop, make 12 Continuous Crossover Loops (4 row).
b. Once completed, leave 4" of bare wire. Cut the bare wire, and bring it up between the first two petals made.
c. Pull it back down between two petals on the opposite side of the flower.
d. DON'T twist.

Center (round)
Make 1 (yellow)
1-bead basic, 14 rows
a. Since you have an even number of rows, you will end at the top basic wire. Leave 4" of bare wire, and cut from spool.
b. DON'T cut the top basic wire.
c. Bend all of the wires backwards 90°.
d. DON'T twist.

Sepals
Make 1 (green)
Make 8 continuous 1/2" loops.

Leaves

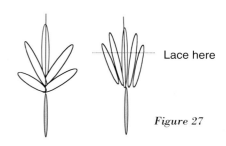

Lace here

Figure 27

Make 2 (green)
2" basic, 11 rows
a. Make the first 3 rows as usual.
b. Take row 4 up the side, but stop 1/2" from the top.
c. Turn and bead down to the bottom, then up the other side. Turn 1/2" from the top.
d. Repeat, but this time stop 1/2" from the previous row.
e. Leave 3 wires, twist, and tape.
f. Lace the leaf, and then bend the loose tips outward (fig. 27).

Assembly

Large Ox-Eye Daisy
1. Lightly tape the stem wire.
2. Place the flower center over the middle of the petals. Push the center down, with the wires passing between petals. Pull the wires to the middle of the back, and twist several times with the petal wires.
3. Using assembly wire, attach the flower to the end of the stem wire. Cut the petal wires to different lengths. Push the sepals up under the blossom. Wire the sepals in place.
4. Arrange the leaves at attractive places on the stem. Wire them in place.
5. Tape the entire stem.

Black-Eyed Susan
1. Petals (yellow)—Make the same as the daisy.

2. Center (dark brown or black)—1-bead basic, 10 rows. Make the same as the daisy.
3. Stamens—Make the same as the daisy.
4. Leaves—2" basic, 11 rows, (pointed top, pointed bottom).

Coneflower
1. Petals—(pink) Make the same as the daisy.
2. Center—(brown) 1-bead basic, 20 rows.
After completing row 7, bend both wires backwards to about 80°. Continue beading, positioning each row so that you are forming a cup (fig. 19, page 14). End the same as the daisy.
3. Stamens—Make the same as the daisy.
4. Leaves—2 1/2" basic, 11 rows (pointed top, pointed bottom).

Coral Bean

This tall spike of blooms is a great way to add height to your bouquet. If you can find colored floral tape, a red stem adds even more interest to this piece.

Materials Needed

- *2 hanks of red or deep coral pink beads*
- *1/2 hank of green beads*
- *1 strand of yellow beads*
- *26-gauge beading wire*
- *28-gauge gold wire (for the stamens)*
- *30- or 34-gauge wire (for lacing and assembly)*
- *18" of 16-gauge stem wire*
- *1/2" green floral tape*

Buds

Make 4 (red)
- a. Leaving 2" of bare wire before and after, make two 1" Continuous Loops.
- b. Twist the loops into a spiral.

Make 4 (red)
- a. Leaving 2" of bare wire before and after, make two 2" Continuous Loops.
- b. Twist the loops into a spiral.

Make 4 (red) (pointed top, round bottom)
1/4" basic, 7 rows (Twist into a spiral.)

Make 4 (red) (pointed top, round bottom)
1/2" basic, 7 rows (Twist into a spiral.)

Petals (round top, round bottom) (Lace all of the petals.)

Make 4 (red)
1/2" basic, 13 rows (Leave 3 wires, and twist.)

Make 4 (red)
3/4" basic, 13 rows (Leave 3 wires, and twist.)

Make 4 (red)
1" basic, 13 rows (Leave 3 wires, and twist.)

Make 4 (red)
1 1/4" basic, 13 rows (Leave 3 wires, and twist.)

Sepals

Make 16 (red)
Leaving 2" of bare wire before and after, make four 8-bead Continuous Loops (buds)

Make 8 (red)
Leaving 2" of bare wire before and after, make four 12-bead Continuous Loops (small petals)

Make 8 (red)
Leaving 2" of bare wire before and after, make four 16-bead Continuous Loops (large petals)

Stamens

Make 48 (yellow)
- a. Cut 6" of gold wire.
- b. Add 3 beads.
- c. Fold it in half, and twist the entire length.

Leaves (pointed top, round bottom)

Make 3 (green)
3-bead basic, 15 rows
- a. Add 1 bead to the basic wire on each row after row 7.
- b. Leave 3 wires, twist, and tape.

Assembly

1. Lightly tape the stem wire.

2. Apply a sepal to the base of each bud, and twist the wires.

3. Hold a pencil along the back basic wire, and bend each petal into a tube. Where the two laced edges meet, use lacing wire to connect the edges and secure the tube.

4. Slip 3 stamens into each tube. Position them so that they extend about 1/4" past the tip. Add the appropriate size sepal, and twist the wires.

5. Begin at the tip of the stem wire. Use assembly wire to attach the 4 smallest buds.

Allowing 1" between rows, attach the rest of the buds and blooms (4 at a time). Bend the two upper rows upward. Bend the rest of the rows downward.

6. Stack the 3 leaves together. Beginning 1/2" from the beads, twist the stems together. Slide the leaves into a fan shape. Tape the twisted area. Wire this in place 2" to 3" below the bottom bloom.

7. Tape the entire stem with green floral tape.

Queen Anne's Lace

Late summer in Ohio provides us with acres of this delicate beauty. Who can resist the lacey appearance and the aromatec smell of wild carrots?

Materials Needed

1/2 hank of white beads
4 strands of light green beads
1 red bead
30-gauge white wire
26-gauge beading wire
30- to 34-gauge wire (assembly)
18" of 16-gauge stem wire
1/2" green floral tape

Flowerets

Make 35 (white beads on white wire)

    a. Leaving 4" of bare wire, make four 7-bead Continuous Loops.

    b. Leave 4" of bare wire, and twist lightly.

    c. On the last floweret, thread a single red bead onto the wire. Bring the wire over the top of the flower. Center the red bead.

    d. Bring the wire back down, and twist lightly.

Sepals

Make 4 (green)

    a. Leave 3" of bare wire.

    b. Make 3 Continuous Loops. The first is a 1/2" loop. The second requires 1" of beads. And, the third is 1/2" again.

    c. Leave 3" of bare wire, and cut.

    d. Put 1/2" of beads on each wire, and twist.

Make 4 (green)

    a. Leave 3" of bare wire.

    b. Make 3 Continuous Loops. The first is a 1" loop. The second requires 2" of beads. And, the third is 1" again.

    c. Leave 3" of bare wire, and cut.

    d. Put 1" of beads on each wire, and twist up to the loops.

Leaves

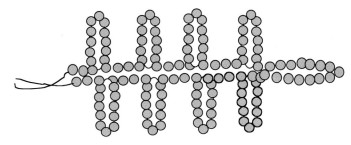

Figure 28

Make 2 (green)

    a. Leave 3" of bare wire.

    b. Make a 1" loop.

    c. Leave 1/2" of beads.

    d. Make another 1" loop.

    e. Repeat until you have 4 loops with 1/2" of beads between them.

    f. Make a 2" loop (tip of leaf).

    g. Make a 1" loop. Leave 1/2" of beads, and then make the next 1" loop. Continue until you have another set of 4 loops with 1/2" beaded spacers.

    h. Cut 3" bare wire, and add 1/2" of beads to each bare end (fig. 28). Twist the wires.

    i. Pinch all of the loops closed, and twist the beads on all of the loops and stem. This gives them a lacier appearance.

Assembly

1. Lightly tape the stem wire.

2. This is a flat-topped flower. Therefore, when assembling flower groups, put the flowerets face down on a smooth surface. Bring the wires toward the center, and adjust the length of each wire to insure that the flowerets remain flat. Once they are in position, twist the wires lightly. Make 4 groups of 3 flowerets. Make 4 groups of 4 flowerets. Make 1 group of 7 flowerets (the one floweret with the red bead should be in the center, and the other six should completely surround it).

3. Arrange the groups as shown in fig. 29. Bring the wires together, and twist. Use assembly wire to attach the flower to the end of the stem. Pull the wires away from the stem, and cut them to different lengths, so that they will taper when pulled back down. Tape this area lightly.

4. Attach the 4 large sepals directly below the flower. Bend them upwards. Attach the 4 small sepals in the spaces between the large sepals. Bend them downwards.

5. Wire the two leaves at attractive distances from the flower. Tape the entire stem.

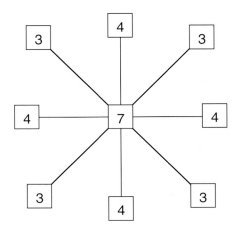

Figure 29

Harvest Lily

This little wild lily blooms so late in the season its leaves often whither before the blooms appear. Therefore, the leaves are done in either tan or transparent gold beads.

Materials Needed

7 to 8 strands of medium or dark purple beads
2 strands of green beads
3 strands of tan beads
1 strand of white beads
1 strand of yellow beads
26-gauge beading wire
30- to 34-gauge assembly wire
Four 18" pieces of 18-gauge stem wire
1/2" green floral tape

Petals (pointed top, round bottom)
  Make 18 (purple)
  1" basic, 5 rows (Reduce to 2 wires.)
  Make 9 (white)
  4-bead basic, 3 rows (Reduce to 2 wires.)

Buds (pointed top, round bottom) (After completion, twist the petal into a spiral.)
  Make 1 (purple)
  3/4" basic, 7 rows (Reduce to 2 wires.)
  Make 1 (green)
  3/4" basic, 7 rows (Reduce to 2 wires.)
  Make 1 (green)
  1/2" basic, 5 rows (Reduce to 2 wires.)

Pistil
  Make 3 (yellow)
  Leaving 2" of bare wire, make one 1" 4-row Crossover Loop, cut wires, and twist.

Leaves (pointed top, round bottom)
  Make 2 (tan)
  1" basic, 11 rows (Leave 3 wires, and twist.)
  Make 2 (tan and green)
  3" basic, 3 rows
      a. String the tan beads, leaving 4" of bare wire, and make your basic loop.
      b. String 3" of green beads on the basic wire.
      c. Complete the next 2 rows with tan (green center, tan on the outside).
      d. Leave 3 wires, and twist.

Assembly

1. Cut one of the stem wires into three 6" pieces (bud stems). Lightly tape the top 4" of all 6 stem wires.

2. Tape a bud to the end of each short wire.

3. Use assembly wire to attach 1 pistil, 3 small white petals, and 6 purple petals to the end of each long wire. Tape each down to the previous tape line.

4. Hold all 6 stems together with the flower and bud bases even. Tightly wrap them together with assembly wire, 1" above the tape line. Attach the two tan leaves at the same point. Tape down the stem about 6", and attach the two bi-color leaves opposite each other. Finish taping.

5. Bend the flowers and buds outward. Twist the bi-color leaves into spirals, and bend them into "withered" shapes.

$\mathcal{B}$leeding $\mathcal{H}$eart

My grandfather's garden always included several of these delicate beauties. To this day, I have carried on the same tradition. Now I will never be without one, regardless of the season.

Materials Needed

1 hank of pink or white beads
4 strands of white beads
   (inserts)
5 strands of green beads
26-gauge beading wire
30-gauge assembly wire
18" of 16-gauge stem wire
14" of 16-gauge stem wire
1/2" green floral tape

Petals (round top, round bottom)

Make 20 (pink or white)
1-bead basic, 13 rows
a. After row 3, bend the basic wire and the basic loop backwards to an approximate 70° position (fig. 30). Continue beading until you complete row 12. (You will be forming a cup.)
b. At the end of row 12, you will be at the top basic wire. Add 4 beads to the basic wire. Bead up and back down these beads. (This will form a 3-row tab on the lip of the cup.) Complete row 13.
c. Reduce to 1 wire, and twist lightly. You now have a "coonskin cap."
d. Find something small and flat—like a Popsicle® stick—and place it inside the cup.
e. Hold it tightly against the basic wire, and pinch the cup flat.
f. Bend the tab and the tip of the cup outward.

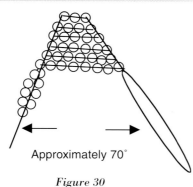

Approximately 70°

Figure 30

Inserts (round top, round bottom)

Make 10 (white)

1/2" basic, 5 rows

    a. After completing row 4, add 4 beads to the basic wire.

    b. Bead up and then down the 4 beads, as in the petals.

    c. Complete row 5.

    d. Reduce to 1 wire, and twist lightly. This is shaped like an elongated figure 8.

Buds

Make 1 (pink and white)

    a. Cut 8" of wire. Center 2" of pink beads, and make a loop.

    b. Add more beads to form the Crossover Loop. Begin with 3/4" of pink, add 1/2" of white, and end with 3/4" of pink. Position the beads so that the bud is white on the tips.

    c. Twist it into a spiral.

Make 1 (pink and white)

    a. Cut 8" of wire. Center 1 1/2" of pink beads, and make a loop.

    b. In the same manner, form the next Crossover Loop. Begin with 1/2" of pink, add 1/2" of white, and end with 1/2" of pink. Position the beads so that the bud is white on the tips.

    c. Twist it into a spiral.

Make 1 (pink)

    a. Leaving 2" of wire before and after, form a 1" Crossover Loop.

    b. Twist it into a spiral.

Leaves (pointed top and bottom)

Make 2 (green) (right)

1" basic, 9 rows

    a. After row 7, bead up the right side to 1/2" from the top.

    b. Turn and bead back down to the bottom.

    c. Reduce to 2 wires, and twist.

    d. Lace the leaf, 1/2" below the folded tip.

    e. Bend the tip outward.

Make 2 (green) (left)

1" basic, 9 rows

    a. After completing row 7, bead up the left side to 1/2" from the top.

    b. Turn and bead back down to the bottom.

    c. Reduce to 2 wires, and twist.

    d. Lace the leaf 1/2" below the folded tip.

    e. Bend the tip outward.

Make 2 (green) (center)

1" basic, 11 rows

    a. After row 7, bead up the right side to 1/2" from the top.

    b. Turn and bead back down to the bottom.

    c. Bead up the left side to 1/2" from the top.

    d. Turn and bead back down to the bottom.

    e. Reduce to 2 wires, and twist.

    f. Lace the leaf 1/2" below the folded tips.

    g. Bend the tips outward.

Assembly

1. Lightly tape the stem wires.

2. Using 2 flattened petals and one insert, slide a pink petal over each "shoulder" of the white insert. Hold all 3 wires together, and twist. Tape lightly. Assemble each of the 10 flowers in the same manner.

3. On the 18" stem wire, tape the smallest bud to the tip. Tape down 1 1/4", and add the next largest bud. Tape down 1 1/4", and add the last bud. Continue in the same manner, adding 5 flowers to the stem. Set aside.

4. On the 14" stem, tape 5 flowers at 1 1/4" intervals.

5. Put the 2 stems together, and secure the lower 4" with wire.

6. Form 2 leaf groups. Stack 1 each of all 3 leaf types. About 1" from the beads, twist the wires and tape the stem.

7. Adjust them so that the large (center) leaf is in the middle and the right and left leaves have their bent tips on the outside of the group.

8. Position them below the "V" of the main stem, and wire them in place. Tape the stem.

Garden Tulip

There is something so neat and pretty about these little Dutch beauties. I think every arrangement deserves a couple!

Materials Needed

1 hank of petal-color beads
1 hank of green beads
1/2 strand of yellow beads
6" of black or brown beads
26-gauge beading wire
30- to 34-gauge wire (for lacing)
Two 9" pieces of 18- or 20-gauge
   stem wire (to stiffen leaves)
16" of 16-gauge (or heavier) stem
   wire
1/2" green floral tape

Petals (round top, round bottom)
   Make 6 (petal color)
   1/2" basic, 21 rows (Leave 3 wires, and twist.)

Leaves (pointed top, round bottom)
   Make 2 (green)
   4" basic, 19 rows
      a. Use one of the 9" pieces of wire, and then use Stem Stiffening Method 1 to strengthen.
      b. Leave 3 wires, and twist.

Pistil
   Make 1 (yellow)
      a. Cut a 10" piece of wire, and mark the center.

   b. Put the 30 beads on the wire, push them to the center, and make three 10-bead loops.
   c. Put 1 1/4" of beads on each wire.
   d. Twist the entire length.

Stamens
   Make 6 (black or brown)
      a. Cut 5" of 34-gauge lacing wire. Put 1" of beads on the center of the wire.
      b. Skipping the first bead, thread back through all of the remaining beads.
      c. Twist them together in groups of 2.

Assembly

1. Lace all of the petals.

2. Lightly tape the stem wire.

3. Using assembly wire, attach the pistil and stamens to the top of the stem. Add 3 petals, and wire them in place. Add the other 3 petals below the spaces of the first set. Tape down the entire stem.

4. Position both leaves about 4" from the bottom. Wire them in place. Tape down the stem. You may also bead this stem.

Lily-Flowering Tulip

This striking tulip is so
large that it only takes 3 or
4 flowers to make an
impressive display. However,
it's a little too large for most
bouquets.

Materials Needed

1 1/2 hanks of red beads
3/4 hank of yellow beads
1 hank of green beads
20 black beads
26-gauge beading wire
30- to 34-gauge wire (for lacing)
Six 8" pieces of 28-gauge wire (to
    stiffen petals)
Two 9" pieces of 18- or 20-gauge
    stem wire (to stiffen leaves)
16" of 16-gauge (or heavier) stem wire
1/2" green floral tape

Petals (pointed top, round bottom)
Make 6 (red and yellow)
3" basic, 15 rows
   a. After completing row 9, leave 1 1/2" of red beads close to the petal.
   b. Measure about 3 feet of bare wire, and cut the petal from the spool.
   c. Add enough yellow beads to complete row 10. Add enough yellow beads to come 1 1/2" from the bottom.
   d. Add 1 1/2" of red beads, and complete row 11. Do the same thing for the next 4 rows, but use 1" of red beads for rows 12 and 13, and use 1/2" of red beads for rows 14 and 15.
   e. Leave 3 wires.
   f. Use a 6" piece of 28-gauge wire to stiffen the stem. Use Stem Stiffening Method 2.

Leaves (pointed top, round bottom)
Make 2 (green)
4" basic, 19 rows
   a. Leave 3 wires.
   b. Stiffen the leaves using Stem Stiffening Method 1.

Pistil
Make 1 (black and green)
   a. Cut a 10" piece of wire, and mark the center.
   b. Put the 20 black beads on the wire, push them to the center, and make two 10-bead loops.
   c. Put 3" of green beads on each wire.
   d. Twist the entire length.

Assembly

1. Lightly tape the stem wire.

2. Using assembly wire, attach the pistil to the top of the stem.

3. Add 3 petals, and wire them in place. Attach the second 3 petals below the spaces of the first 3.

4. Position both leaves about 4" from the bottom. Wire the leaves in place. Tape the entire stem.

Daffodil & Narcissus

It seems like all daffodils used to be yellow. Now any combination of yellow and white, pink and white, or pale green can be found. This allows you to make a bright and colorful spring bouquet using just this flower.

Materials Needed

1 hank of yellow beads
1/2 hank of green beads
1 strand of matte yellow beads
26-gauge beading wire
30- to 34-gauge wire (for lacing and assembly)
18" of 16-gauge stem wire*
1/2" green floral tape

*If you plan to use the flowers in a bouquet, use longer stem wires and attach 1 or 2 leaves to each.

Petals (pointed top, round bottom)
Make 12 (yellow)
1" basic, 9 rows (Leave 3 wires, and twist.)

Center Cups
Make 2 (yellow)
    a. Leave 2" of bare wire. Make 12 Continuous Loops using 3 1/2" of beads per loop (1" per loop for narcissus). Leave 2" of bare wire, and cut from spool. Pinch loops closed.

    b. Lace the loops together 1/2" from the tips of the loops (lace across the center for narcissus) (fig. 31).

    c. When you get to the edge, bring the sides together, and lace them in place. Just above the lacing, bend the tips outward.

Pistil
Make 2 (matte yellow)
    a. Using 2" of beads for the first loop, make a single Crossover Loop, and twist wires.

    b. Make 3 Continuous Loops for the narcissus, 1/2" of beads each.

Leaves (pointed top, round bottom)
Make 3 (green)
6" basic, 5 rows
    a. Leave 3 wires, and twist.

    b. Lace each leaf twice.

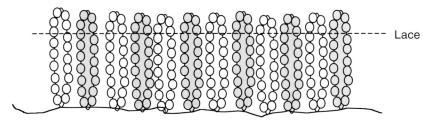

Lace

Once laced, bring the ends of the lacing wire together and twist.
Bring bottom wires together and twist them also.

Figure 31

Assembly

1. Lightly tape the stem wires.

2. Put a pistil into the center of a laced cup. Twist all the wires together.

3. Using assembly wire, attach the center assembly to the top of the stem wire.

4. Still using assembly wire, attach 6 of the petals (3 at a time). Tape down the entire stem. Repeat for the second flower.

5. Two inches from their bottoms, wire the two flowers together.

6. Position all 3 leaves. Wire them in place, and tape.

7. About 1/2" from the flower, bend the flower stems downward.

Pansy

This is such a pretty and cheerful little flower. Choose almost any color you want. You can even leave out the petal shading, if you choose.

Materials Needed

1/2 hank of petal-color beads
1 hank of green beads
1 strand of black beads
12 yellow beads
26-gauge gold or colored beading wire
30- to 34-gauge assembly wire
6" of 16-gauge stem wire
1/2" green floral tape

Petals (round top, round bottom)

Make 2 (petal color)

1-bead basic, 19 rows (Reduce to 2 wires, and twist.)

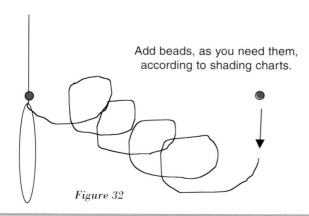

Add beads, as you need them, according to shading charts.

Figure 32

Make 3

1-bead basic, 17 rows

    a. Cut at least 3 feet of bare wire. Use it to form your basic wire and basic loop.

    b. Feed the beads that you need onto the cut end of the wire (fig. 32). For two of the petals, use Shading Chart #1. For the third petal, use Shading Chart #2.

    c. On the even numbered rows, add your shading beads at the beginning of the row. On the odd numbered rows, add the shading beads at the end of the rows.

    d. Complete each row with the petal-color beads.

    e. Reduce to 2 wires, and twist.

Pansy Shading Chart #1		Pansy Shading Chart #2	
Row #		Row #	
1 -	1 black (basic)	1 -	petal color (basic)
2 -	2 black	2 -	petal color
3 -	2 black	3 -	petal color
4 -	3 black	4 -	petal color
5 -	3 black	5 -	petal color
6 -	5 black	6 -	5 black
7 -	5 black	7 -	5 black
8 -	6 black	8 -	6 black
9 -	6 black	9 -	6 black
10 -	7 black	10 -	6 black
11 -	7 black	11 -	6 black + 1 yellow
12 -	7 black	12 -	1 yellow + 6 black
13 -	7 black	13 -	6 black + 2 yellow
14 -	7 black	14 -	2 yellow + 6 black
15 -	7 black	15 -	5 black + 2 yellow
16 -	6 black	16 -	2 yellow + 5 black
17 -	6 black	17 -	4 black + 2 yellow

Buds

Make 1 (petal color)
a. Leave 8" of bare wire. Make 2 Continuous Loops, using 1" of beads for each loop.
b. Leave 8" of bare wire, and cut. Don't twist.
c. Twist the beaded loops into a spiral.

Make 1 (petal color)
a. Leave 8" of bare wire. Make 2 Continuous Loops, using 1 1/2" of beads for each loop.
b. Leave 8" of bare wire, and cut. Don't twist.
c. Twist the beaded loops into a spiral.

Make 1 (petal color)
a. Leave 8" of bare wire. Make 3 Continuous Loops using 2" of beads for each loop.
b. Leave 8" of bare wire, and cut. Don't twist.
c. Twist the beaded loops into a spiral.

Sepals

Make 1 (green)
a. Leave 8" of bare wire. Make 4 Continuous Loops, using 3/4" of beads per loop.
b. Leave 8" of bare wire, and cut.

Make 3 (green)
a. Leave 8" of bare wire. Make 4 Continuous Loops, using 1" of beads per loop.
b. Leave 8" of bare wire, and cut.

Leaves

Make 10 (green)
1 1/2" basic, 3 rows
a. Use 3" of beads to make a loop on both the right and left side of the stem, repeat the procedure using 2 1/2" of beads for each loop (fig. 27, see page 33).
b. Leave 3 wires, and twist.
c. Flatten the loops tight against either side of the 3-row leaf.
d. Lace once across the leaf, making sure to catch 1/4" below the tips of the shortest loops in the lacing.
e. Twist wires, and tape.

Assembly

1. Slip the smallest bud into the smallest sepal. Twist the wires, and tape. Tape a leaf about 2" to 3" from the bud. Assemble the other 2 buds in the same manner. Bend the stems at an angle, about 1/2" from the buds.

2. Hold the 3 shaded petals together with their bases even. Wrap the stems twice with assembly wire.

3. Position the two large petals behind the black shaded petals. Wrap them again with assembly wire.

4. Position the last sepal tight against the back of the flower, and twist all of the wires together.

5. Wire this to the 6" stem wire. Add 2 leaves, one 3" down the stem, the second 1" below the first. Tape the stem.

6. Hold the bloom and buds together in a nosegay. Wrap the bottoms with assembly wire.

7. Add 3 leaves, at the same level, to the wired stem.

8. Drop down 1/2", and add the other 3 leaves. Tape the assembly area.

*Large and lovely!
This flower looks great in
large, tall bouquets.
Choose any shade of pink
or blue, as well as light green
or white.*

Hydrangea

Materials Needed

2 hanks of petal-color beads
1 hank of green beads
1/2 strand of yellow beads
26-gauge beading wire
30- to 34-gauge assembly wire
18" of 1/8" rod for the stem (or 4 to 5
    16-gauge stems taped together)
1/2" green floral tape

Flowerets
Make 30 (petal color)

a. Leave 5" of bare wire.

b. Using 7 beads for the first loops, make four Continuous Triple Loops (six rows across). Simply go around the Continuous Double Loop one more time.

c. Bring the wire up between the first two petals that you made, and then bring it back down between the last two petals constructed.

d. Measure 5" of bare wire, and cut the wire from the spool.

e. Intending to form an "X" in the flower's center with the wire you previously drew across the top, bring the other cut wire back up between the second and third petals. Put 2 yellow beads on the wire.

f. Bring the wire across the top, centering the yellow beads on the top of the flower. Pull the wire down the other side, completing the "X."

g. Pull the wires together, and twist.

Leaves (pointed top, round bottom)
Make 2 (green)
4-bead basic, 37 rows

a. Leave 3 wires, twist, tape, and lace.

b. Make a slight crease down the center of the leaf, and then bend the tip down slightly.

Assembly

1. Lightly tape the stem rod.

2. Make 5 groups of 4 flowerets each. About 1 1/4" from the flowerets, twist the wires and tape lightly.

3. An inch from the top of the taped area, bend the stems 90°. Use assembly wire to connect all five groups to the top of the stem rod. (This should look like a wheel with 5 spokes.)

4. Use the remaining 10 flowerets to form a nosegay. Twist and tape the stems, as in the 4 floweret groups. Drop the nosegay down into the center of the "hub" just constructed. Position the nosegay at an attractive level. Wire it in place. Tape the assembly area.

5. Wire and tape the first leaf 4" from the flower. Drop down 3" to 4", and attach the second leaf. Tape the stem again. Tug the flowerets lightly into position, filling in the empty spaces. (If there are any large gaps that cannot be filled by repositioning, make 1 or 2 more flowerets, drop them into the holes, and tape them in place.)

Gladiola

Tall and graceful, this majestic flower is a must in any large bouquet. Please excuse my fantasy color of navy blue. I needed it to go with my hydrangeas.

Materials Needed

3 hanks of petal-color beads
2 strands of contrasting-color beads (for the stamens)
1/2 hank of green beads
26-gauge beading wire
34-gauge wire (for the pistil and stamens)
18" of 20-gauge stem wire (to stiffen leaf)
30- to 34-gauge assembly wire
24" of 1/8" stem rod
1/2" green floral tape

Petals (round top, pointed bottom)
(Lace all of the petals.)

Make 3 (petal color)
6-bead basic, 21 rows
(Reduce to 2 wires, and twist.)

Make 6 (petal color)
6-bead basic, 19 rows
(Reduce to 2 wires, and twist.)

Make 6 (petal color)
6-bead basic, 17 rows
(Reduce to 2 wires, and twist.)

Make 6 (petal color)
6-bead basic, 15 rows
(Reduce to 2 wires, and twist.)

Make 6 (petal color)
6-bead basic, 13 rows
(Reduce to 2 wires, and twist.)

Make 3 (petal color)
6-bead basic, 11 rows
(Reduce to 2 wires, and twist.)

Buds (pointed tops, round bottoms)
    Make 2 (petal color)
    6-bead basic, 11 rows (Leave 3 wires, and twist.)
    Make 2 (petal color)
    6-bead basic, 9 rows (Leave 3 wires, and twist.)
    Make 2 (green)
    1" basic, 9 rows (Leave 3 wires, and twist.)
    Make 1 (green)
    3/4" basic, 7 rows (Leave 3 wires, and twist.)

Pistil

    Make 5 (petal color and contrasting color)
    a. Cut 8" of 34-gauge wire. Thread 6 beads (petal color) onto the wire, and center them.
    b. Thread one end of the wire back through 5 beads, skipping the one closest to the end of the wire that you are using.
    c. Add 6 beads to the wire, and thread back through the 5 beads furthest from the tip.
    d. Do this once more. Bring the 2 wires together. Slide 1" of beads (contrasting color) onto the two combined wires (fig. 33).

Stamens
    Make 15 (contrasting color)
    a. Cut 6" of 34-gauge wire. String 1 1/4" beads onto the wire.
    b. Thread back through all but 1 bead.
    c. Twist the stamens together in groups of 3.

Sepals (pointed top, round bottom)
Make 20 (green)
    6-bead basic, 7 rows (Leave 3 wires, and twist.)

Leaf (pointed top, round bottom)
    Make 1 (green)
    14" basic, 9 rows
    a. After measuring the basic row, stiffen the leaf with Stem Stiffening Method 1.
    b. Leave 3 wires, and twist.

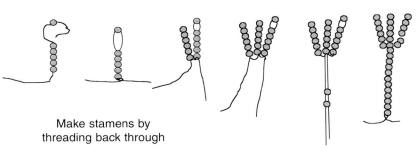

Make stamens by threading back through

Figure 33

Finish by bringing the bottom wires together and threading both through the desired number of beads.

Assembly

1. Lightly tape the stem rod.

2. 3 green buds—Lightly fold each green bud petal in half, lengthwise. Add 2 sepals, twist the wires, and tape.

3. 2 petal-color buds—Lightly fold the colored bud petals in half, lengthwise. Matching the sizes, put 2 bud petals together with edges interlocking, add 2 sepals, twist the wires, and tape.

4. Flowers—Put 1 pistil and 3 stamens together, and twist the wires. Position the 3 smallest petals around the pistil-stamen group, and wrap twice with assembly wire. Add 3 of the next largest petals, and wrap again with assembly wire. Twist all of the wires together, trim them to 2 1/2", and tape. Repeat this process until all 5 flowers are completed.

5. Without cutting the assembly wire between items, use it to attach the smallest green bud to the tip of the stem. Drop down 1 1/2" and (directly below the first) add another green bud, leaving 1" of taped bud stem free.

6. Continue by adding the last green bud, the last 2 colored buds (smallest first), the flowers (smallest to largest), and the leaf in the same manner.

7. Tape the entire stem. Slightly adjust the flowers and buds (one right, one left) down the entire length.

$\mathcal{S}$ ansevieria
(Mother-in-Law's Tongue)

Not my mother-in-law's, of course.

Materials Needed

2 hanks of medium green beads
3/4 hank of pale yellow beads
26-gauge wire
30- to 34-gauge assembly wire
1/2" green floral tape

Leaves (pointed tops, round bottom)
Make 2 of each size
1/2" basic, 9 rows
    a. First use 7 green, measure 4" of bare wire, and cut.
    b. Make the last 2 rows yellow.
    c. Leave 3 wires, and twist.

3/4" basic, 11 rows
    a. First use 7 green, measure 9" of bare wire, and cut.
    b. Make the last 4 rows yellow.
    c. Leave 3 wires, and twist.

3/4" basic, 13 rows
    a. First use 9 green, measure 10" of bare wire, and cut.
    b. Make the last 4 rows yellow.
    c. Leave 3 wires, and twist.

3/4" basic, 15 rows
    a. First use 11 green, measure 11" of bare wire, and cut.
    b. Make the last 4 rows yellow.
    c. Leave 3 wires, and twist.

1" basic, 17 rows
    a. First use 13 green, measure 12" of bare wire, and cut.
    b. Make the last 4 rows yellow.
    c. Leave 3 wires, and twist.

1" basic, 19 rows
    a. First use 15 green, measure 13" of bare wire, and cut.
    b. Make the last 4 rows yellow.
    c. Leave 3 wires, and twist.

1" basic, 21 rows
    a. First use 17 green, measure 14" of bare wire, and cut.
    b. Make the last 4 rows yellow.
    c. Leave 3 wires, and twist.

Assembly

1. Lace all of the leaves once, one third of the way from the tips.

2. Use assembly wire to bind the two smallest leaves together. Continue to add the leaves, smallest to largest.

3. Once you have them all connected, twist all of the stem wires together tightly. Trim the stem to 2" or 3", and tape.

*I*ris

Materials Needed

1 1/4 hanks of petal-color beads
1/2 strand of yellow beads
1/2 hank of green beads
26-gauge beading wire
22-gauge green floral wire (for the leaves)*
30- to 34-gauge assembly wire
18" of 1/8" metal rod (or 4 16-gauge wires
   wired together)
1/2" green floral tape

*10/0 beads will usually slide on the 22-gauge wire.
If you are using smaller beads or the holes are too
small, use a finer gauge wire, and stiffen the leaf
using Stem Stiffening Method 1.

*T*all, straight, and majestic,
the iris always turns heads
with its striking beauty.
Purples, blues, lavenders,
yellows, and white give you a
large choice when choosing
the ideal iris for your display.

Petals (round top, pointed bottom) (Lace all of the petals.)
>**Make 3 (petal color)**
>1/2" basic, 21 rows (Leave 3 wires, and twist.)
>**Make 3 (petal color)**
>3/4" basic, 19 rows (When completed, use Stem Stiffening Method 2.)
>**Make 3 (petal color)**
>1 1/2" basic, 7 rows (Leave 3 wires, and twist.)

Beard
>**Make 3 (yellow)**
>a. Leave 3" of bare wire. Make a single loop of 3" of yellow beads.
>b. Leave 3" of bare wire, cut, and twist.
>c. Pinch the loop closed, and twist into a spiral.

Leaf (pointed top, round bottom)
>**Make 1 (green)**
>8" basic, 9 rows on 22-gauge floral wire (Leave 3 wires, and twist.)

Assembly

1. Lightly tape the stem wire.

2. Wrinkle the edges of the 3 large and 3 small petals by bending the outer rows (similar to crimping the edges of a pie crust).

3. Using assembly wire, attach all 3 of the medium petals (the ones that have stiffened stems) to the top of the stem wire, making sure that the back sides are facing inward. Cup them top to bottom, and side to side. Leave the petals pointed upward. Set aside.

4. Matching the bottoms, lay a beard along the center of the right side of a large petal. Lightly twist the wires. Use a short piece of wire to tack the beard in place. (Push the wire up from the underside of the petal, go through just the lower side of the beard loop, about 1/4" from the tip. Thread the wire back through to the underside of the petal. Twist the 2 ends together, trim to 1/8", and tuck the wire out of sight.)

5. Place one of the small petals over the top of the beard, front side down. Match the bottoms, and twist the three wires. Mold the sides of the small petal around the beard, cocoon fashion. Bend the tip of the small petal up and back to reveal about 1/2 of the beard. Repeat with the other 2 sets.

6. Positioning the large petal assemblies below the spaces between the medium petals, use assembly wire to attach all 3 large petal assemblies to the stem. Cut the exposed petal wires to different lengths so that they feather down the stem and don't create a lump. Tape down the stem.

7. Use assembly wire to attach the leaf at an attractive position, about 7" below the bloom.

8. Tape the stem again. Rub and smooth the tape to seal the wax.

Hibiscus

This flower grows on a shrub that brings an air of elegance to any patio. Choose red, pink, orange, or yellow for a realistic effect.

Materials Needed

1 hank of pink beads
1/2 hank of dark green beads
10 yellow beads
26-gauge beading wire
30- to 34-gauge assembly wire
18" of 16-gauge stem wire
1/2" green floral tape
1/2" brown floral tape

Petals (flat top, pointed bottom) (Lace all of the petals.)

Make 5 (petal color)

1-bead basic, 23 rows

a. Use 8 beads each for rows 2 and 3.

b. Push the top down tight against the center bead, forming a short, flat, sideways oval.

c. After row 3, begin forming the pointed bottom. Keep the top flat by continuously pushing the top beads down tight against the previous row (fig. 34).

d. Leave 3 wires, and twist.

Stamens

Make 10 (yellow)

a. Cut 6" of wire

b. Fold it in half, and add 1 yellow bead to the center.

c. Twist the entire length.

Leaves (pointed top, pointed bottom) (Lace all of the leaves.)

Make 4 (green)

8-bead basic, 15 rows

a. Leave 3 wires, and twist.

b. After the leaves are completed, tape the leaf stems with 1/2" green floral tape.

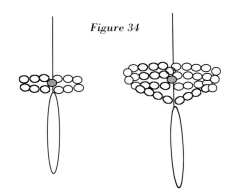

Figure 34

Assembly

1. Lightly tape the stem wire with brown floral tape.

2. Gather all of the stamens together with the top beads even. Pinch tightly 1/2" from the beads. Twist all of the bottom wires together. Use assembly wire to attach this group to the end of the brown stem, leaving 1 3/4" of the stamen assembly above the stem.

3. Attach all 5 of the petals, one at a time, making sure to overlap slightly on one side only. Trim the exposed wires to different lengths, and tape down the stem.

4. Make a circle with your thumb and forefinger. Push the flower down into the circle to form a trumpet shape. Push the centers of the petals outward to widen the center of the trumpet. Flare the petal tips outward. Spread the top 1/2" of the stamen assembly into a starburst.

5. Wrinkle the edges of the leaves slightly. Use assembly wire to attach the leaves to the stem at 1 1/4" intervals on alternate sides of the stem. Be sure to leave about 1/2" of the green, taped wire showing.

6. Re-tape the entire main stem with brown tape. Rub the stem to seal the wax.

African Violet

This is described as everyone's favorite houseplant. However, once you've killed as many as I have, this beaded beauty comes as a welcome addition to the windowsill.

Materials Needed

1/2 hank of petal-color beads
2 hanks of green beads
1/2 strand of yellow beads
26-gauge beading wire
30- to 34-gauge wire (for lacing)
1/2" green floral tape

Flowers

Make 17 (petal color)

   a. Leave 5" of bare wire. Use 3/4" of beads for each inner loop.

   b. Make 4 Double Continuous Loops, or use 4-row Crossover Loops for a more compact look. Leave 5" of bare wire, and cut.

   c. Bring one of the bottom wires up between the first two petals made.

   d. Pull the wire back down between the last two petals made.

   e. Intending to form an "X" in the center of the flower, bring the other wire up between the two side petals.

   f. Put 2 yellow beads on the wire, and center them on top of the flower.

   g. Pull the wire back down on the opposite side.

   h. Pull the two wires together, and twist lightly.

Buds

Make 4 (petal color)

   a. Leave 5" of bare wire. Use 3/4" of beads for each loop.

   b. Make 4 Continuous Loops. Leave 5" of bare wire, and cut.

   c. Pull the two wires together, and twist lightly.

   d. Pinch the loops closed, and cup them toward the center.

Leaves (pointed top, round bottom) (Lace all of the leaves.)

Make 3 (green)
1/2" basic, 25 rows (Leave 3 wires, and twist.)

Make 3 (green)
1/2" basic, 27 rows (Leave 3 wires, and twist.)

Assembly

1. Position the flowers in groups of 4. About 1" from the blooms, twist the wires lightly. The last group will have 1 bloom and 4 buds. Position all of the groups together to form a nosegay. Twist the lower 3" together.

2. Use assembly wire to attach 3 leaves to the lower 3" of the flowers. Drop down 1/4" and attach the last 3 leaves. Trim the wires to the same length, and cover the assembly area with green floral tape.

Oriental Poppy

Materials Needed
(1 flower, 1 bud, 2 leaves)

1 hank of petal-color beads
3 strands of navy or black beads
1 hank of light green beads
26-gauge beading wire
22-gauge (for 10/0 beads) or
    24-gauge (for 11/0 beads) wire
    (for leaves)
Four 16" pieces of 16-gauge stem
    wires, or two 16" pieces of
    1/8" stem wires
1/2" green floral tape

What a wonderful flower! You can make this one in red, orange, pink, white, or pale yellow. You can also omit the dark area on the petal for some varieties.

Petals (flat top, pointed bottom) (See fig. 34, page 59)
Make 6 (petal color)
1-bead basic, 23 rows

a. Cut 6 feet of bare wire. Make a basic wire and loop as you normally would, but without the beads. You will be adding the beads, as needed, from the opposite end of the wire. (If you have trouble with the added beads sliding off the cut end of the wire, clip your hemostats on the end of the wire.)

b. Put 1 bead on the basic wire and 16 on the cut wire.

c. Use 8 beads for row 2, and use 8 beads for row 3. Push the rows down tight against the center bead, forming a very short, wide petal. As you work, keep the top of the petal flat and gradually work the bottom to a point.

d. For the next 10 rows, begin each even-numbered row with 4 navy beads, and end each odd-numbered row with 4 navy beads. (Use the petal-color beads to complete the rows.)

e. Finish the rest of the petals with the petal-color beads.

f. Leave 3 wires, and twist.

Stamens
Make 1 (navy)
Using 2" of beads per loop, make 20 Continuous Loops.

Center Pod (String the beads on green wire.)
Make 1 (petal color, green, or navy)
Combination of beehive and basket bottom.
Note: Since you want the wires to show on the top of the pod, you will be displaying what is normally the back side of this piece.

a. Cut three 6" pieces of green wire. Hold them together and, leaving 3" of bare wire overlapping the center, wrap the beaded spool wire twice around the center of the cut pieces.

b. Spread the wires open like the spokes of a wheel. You will now bead around this by placing the required number of beads between the spokes and wrapping the wire around each spoke (fig. 35).

c. Since this is "back side up," bring your wire under and around the spoke each time you wrap it.

d. Place beads as follows (When the number of beads decreases, bend wires backwards to accommodate the shorter distances):

Round #1—Put 1 bead between each spoke.
Round #2—Put 2 beads between each spoke.
Round #3—Put 3 beads between each spoke.
Round #4—Put 5 beads between each spoke.
Round #5—Put 6 beads between each spoke.
Round #6—Put 6 beads between each spoke.
Round #7—Put 5 beads between each spoke.
Round #8—Put 5 beads between each spoke.
Round #9—Put 5 beads between each spoke.
Round #10—Put 4 beads between each spoke.

e. Straighten the wires. Shape them into a smooth, round pod.

f. Bring the wires together under the center, and twist (fig. 35).

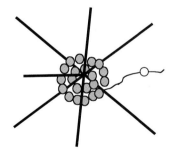

Top view

Figure 35

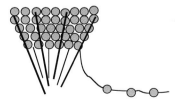

Side view

Sepals and Bud

Make 6 (green)

1/2" basic, 11 rows

    a. After completing row 5, bend the top basic wire backwards 90°.

    b. Once complete, DON'T cut the top basic wire on 3 of these.

    c. Leave 3 wires, and twist.

Leaves

Make 2 (green)

    a. Use 22- or 24-gauge wire to make these as stiff as possible. Leave 3" of bare wire.

    b. Make the following series of loops (leaving 1/2" of beads between each of the loops):

Make 3 loops using 2" of beads per loop.

Make 3 loops using 1 1/2" of beads per loop.

Make 7 loops using 1" of beads per loop.

Make 3 loops using 1 1/2" of beads per loop.

Make 3 loops using 2" of beads per loop.

    c. Leave 1" of beads and 2" of bare wire, and cut.

    d. Put 1" of beads on the beginning bare wire. Put the wires together, and twist.

    e. Fold the circle closed, and twist the entire length.

    f. Give the large individual loops a half twist.

Assembly

Using either one heavy or two light stem wires, wired together, lightly tape the stems.

Bud

1. Using the 3 bud/sepal pieces that still have the long basic wires intact, hold the tips together, and twist the top wires.

2. Trim the wires to 1/2", and tuck them inside the bud.

3. Bring the bottom wires together, and twist.

4. Use assembly wire to attach this to the top of one of the stems. Drop down about 4", and wire a leaf in place. Lightly tape down the stem.

Flower

1. Allowing 1/2" of the stem to go up inside, use assembly wire to attach the pod to the top of the second stem wire. Keep the assembly wire attached.

2. Directly below the pod, wrap the 20-loop stamen wire around the stem. Keep it as close to the pod as possible. Wrap any trailing ends with the assembly wire.

3. Add the 6 petals, 3 at a time, with the second row directly under the spaces of the first row. Center a sepal under each of the lower petals, and again use the assembly wire to secure these.

4. Drop down about 4", and wire the other leaf in place.

5. Hold the bud and flower stems together, and decide where they should be joined, if at all. If you are joining them, mark each stem where they will be coming together. DON'T join at this time.

Bead the Stems

1. String about 5 feet of green beads.

2. Do the bud FIRST. Wrap the beads down to your mark. End here by wrapping the bare wire several times around the stem, as close to the beads as possible.

3. Then spiral the wire down a few inches before cutting.

4. Do the same thing to the flower stem. DON'T cut the wire when you reach the mark. Once you reach the mark, use another piece of wire to tightly attach the two stems together.

5. Continue beading down the stem (now going around both stem wires). Stop at least 1" to 3" from the bottom. End as before.

6. Cut the wire, and cover all exposed wire with floral tape.

Tiger Lily

Change the colors and mix them up to make all sorts of garden lilies. This same pattern, completed in white, is the perfect Easter lily. Bend the petals to produce your favorite lily shape. Even change the leaves to a pair of iris leaves to produce other varieties.

Materials Needed

3 hanks of petal-color beads
1 hank of brown beads
3 1/2 hanks of medium green beads
1/2 strand of yellow beads
26-gauge beading wire
30- to 34-gauge assembly wire
Four 18" pieces of 16-gauge, or
    heavier, stem wire
1/2" green floral tape

Bud (pointed top, round bottom)
Make 4 (solid petal color)
3" basic, 5 rows (Leave 3 wires, and twist.)

Petals (pointed top, round bottom) (Lace all of the petals.)
Make 18 (For spots, mix 3 parts petal color with 1 part brown before stringing.)
2 1/2" basic, 13 rows (Leave 3 wires, and twist.)

Stamens

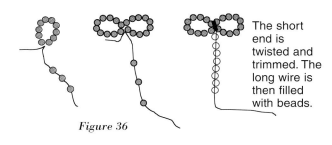

Figure 36

The short end is twisted and trimmed. The long wire is then filled with beads.

Make 18 (petal color and brown)
a. Place 24 brown beads on wire strung with petal-color beads. Leave 1" of bare wire.
b. Make two 12-bead loops.
c. Thread the 1" of bare wire down through one of the loops, and pull it tight. Trim it off close to the underside of the loops.

d. Slide 2" of petal-color beads close to the loops. Leave 2" of bare wire, and cut.
e. Twist the stamens together in groups of 2 (fig. 36).
f. Shape into a "T."

Pistil
Make 3 (yellow and petal color)
a. Cut 12" of bare wire. Put 24 yellow beads on the wire. Leave 4 1/2" of bare wire.
b. Make three 8-bead loops. Put 2 1/2" of petal-color beads on each of the wires. Twist the entire length of both wires.
c. Bend all 3 loops down to form a yellow knob on the tip.
d. Twist each pistil together with 6 stamens (three 2-stamen groups).

Leaves (pointed top, round bottom) (Lace all of the leaves.)
Make 12 (green)
4" basic, 9 rows (Leave 3 wires, and twist.)
Make 4 (green)
2" basic, 7 rows (Leave 3 wires, and twist.)

Assembly

1. Lightly tape the top 4" of the stem wires.
2. Hold all of the buds tightly together. Twist them into a spiral. Use assembly wire to attach the bud to the end of one of the stem wires.
3. Use assembly wire to attach a stamen-pistil group to the end of another wire. Add 3 petals, and wire in place. Place the next 3 petals below the spaces of the first 3, and wire in place. Tape over the assembly area. Repeat for the other 2 flowers.
4. Beginning tight against the base of the flower, bead 3" of the stem with medium green.

Beginning where the beading ends, wire all of the stems together.
5. Use assembly wire to attach the 4 small leaves where the stems meet. Attach the rest of the leaves, 2 leaves at a time, opposite each other, every 1 1/4" down the stem.
6. Finish beading the stem. Tape over any exposed wires.

$\mathcal{L}$iatris

(Gayfeather)

$\mathcal{T}$his eye catcher makes a great focal point or filler. A full bouquet of these, in purple and white, makes a stunning upright display.

Materials Needed

1 hank of petal-color beads
1/2 hank of green beads
26- or 28-gauge beading wire
26- or 28-gauge colored beading wire
16" of 16-gauge or heavier stem wire
1/2" green floral tape

Petals

a. Begin by stringing the entire hank of petal-color beads onto the colored beading wire. Leave 3" of bare wire.

b. Using 1" of beads for each loop, make 14" of Continuous Loops, leaving 3 beads between each loop.

c. Continue by making another 14" of Continuous Loops, using 3/4" of beads per loop, with 3 beads between loops.

d. Finish with 7" of 1/2" Continuous Loops, again with 3 beads between the loops. Leave 3" of bare wire.

Leaves

a. String the entire 1/2 hank of green beads onto the green wire. Leave 3" of bare wire.

b. Make 6" of Continuous Loops, using 2" of beads per loop and 3 beads between loops.

c. Make another 6" of loops, using 3" of beads per loop and the 3 bead spacers.

Assembly

1. Lightly tape the stem wire.

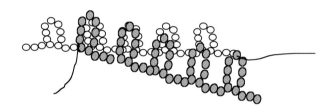

Join the strands of petal loops and leaf loops so that they overlap.

Figure 38

2. Halfway along the area of the smallest petal loops (about 3 1/2" from the bottom), connect the length of leaf loops by twisting the bare green wire, closest to the shortest leaf loops, around the beaded wire (fig. 38).

3. Hold the large petal's end loop, so that the base is even with the top of the stem wire. Wrap the unbeaded wire around and down the stem.

4. Begin wrapping the petal loops (with connected leaf loops) around and down the stem by twirling the stem wire. Keep the rows tight against each other so none of the taped stem shows through. Go all the way down, until you run out of loops. Then wrap the bare wire around the stem. Cover the bare wire with floral tape.

Calla Lily

As much as I love the calla, you would think I would be able to grow one. Unfortunately, I think one of the critters in my yard also enjoys these delicate beauties. So, for now, I'll have to keep to the beaded variety. For a realistic plant, choose white, pink, lavender, red, orange, or yellow for your petal.

Materials Needed

1 hank of petal-color beads
1 1/4 hank of green beads
3 strands of yellow beads
24-gauge beading wire
30- to 34-gauge wire (for lacing and assembly)
Two 16" pieces of 16-gauge or heavier stem wire
1/2" green floral tape

Petal (pointed top, round bottom)
Make 1 (petal color)
2-bead basic, 59 rows
  a. String the entire hank of petal-color beads before you begin.
  b. After row 50, begin adding an extra bead to the basic wire.
  c. Lace 3 times, once across the center and twice more in an "X" that passes through the center.
  d. Begin on the upper right side, and end on the lower left.
  e. Leave 3 wires, and twist.

Pistil
Make 1 (yellow)
  a. Lightly tape your stem wires together.
  b. Make a small disk, 1-bead basic, 3 rows.
  c. Cut the basic loop open, but DON'T cut from the spool!
  d. Position the disk on the top of the stem wire. Bend the wires down against the stem. Hold the disk tightly in place, and bead down the stem.

  e. Use the entire strand of yellow, approximately 3" of beading.
  f. Wrap 2" of bare wire down the stem. Cut the wire, and tape lightly over it.

Leaves (pointed top, round bottom)
Make 2 (green and yellow)
1" basic, 31 rows
  a. Use one of the 9" pieces of wire and Stem Stiffening Method 2 to strengthen the leaves.
  b. To get the random yellow spots, mix 2 strands of yellow beads with 1 hank of green beads before you begin stringing. If you have a bead spinner, this is a good time to use it.
  c. Add 1 extra bead to the basic wire each time you get to the top of the leaf. This will give you a nice, sharp point.
  d. Leave 3 wires, and twist.

Assembly

1. String the remaining 1/4 hank of green beads. Bead 1" of the stem wires of both leaves. Set them aside.

2. On the pistil, beginning at the bottom of the yellow beads, bead down 1/2" with green. DON'T cut the wire!

3. Gently curl the lower edges of the petal forward. Put a pencil along the center front, and tighten the curl around the pencil. Using lacing wire, tack the two edges together where the lower legs of the lacing "X" come together. Slip the petal over the

top of the beaded pistil. Position it so that the base of the petal is exactly even with the bottom of the green beads. Use assembly wire to secure the petal to the stem.

4. Continue beading down the stem for another 3". DON'T cut the wire!

5. Wire the 2 leaves in place, directly below the beads. Continue beading down the stem for at least another 1/2". Wrap several inches of bare wire down the stem. Cut the wire. Tape over any exposed ends.

Hyacinth

Without a doubt, this is our most fragrant early bloomer. I love the smell so much that I add a drop of hyacinth oil to the pot of each beaded replica as the finishing touch. The colors I see most often in our local gardens are purple, pink, lavender, and white.

Materials Needed

2 hanks of petal-color beads

1 hank of green

26 yellow beads

24-gauge beading wire

30-gauge green assembly wire

Four 9" pieces of 20-gauge stem wire (for stiffening leaves)

Two 12" pieces of 16-gauge stem wire

1/2" green floral tape

Flowers
Make 26 (petal color)

a. Leave 2" of bare wire. Using 2" of beads per loop, make six 3-row Crossover Loops. Be sure to pinch the loops closed before beading up the front and down the back. (Remember, on a 3-row Crossover Loop, there is bare wire down the back of each petal.)

b. Once completed, leave 3" of bare wire, and cut. Bring the 3" end across the bottom, up between the first two petals made, and then down between the last two petals made. Pull it tight.

c. Intending to form an "X" in the center of the flower, bring the end back up between two of the side petals, add 1 yellow bead, and bring the wire back down on the opposite side.

d. Twist the wires, and tape them lightly with floral tape that has been cut to 1/4" width.

e. Halfway along the length of the petals, bend them outward. Then pull them all toward the center to form a trumpet shape.

Leaves (pointed top, round bottom)
Make 4 (green)
6" basic, 7 rows

a. Use Stem Stiffening Method 1 to stiffen each leaf.

b. Leave 3 wires, and twist.

Assembly

1. Lightly tape the stem wires together.

2. Using assembly wire, attach a single flower to the end of the stem. Make sure that the beaded portion touches the end of the stem wire. Wrap the wire down about 3/4". Trim the excess flower wire, but DON'T cut the assembly wire.

3. Bend each of the remaining flower stems about 3/8" from the blossoms. Hold the bent portion of the next flower against the stem. Wire it in place so that the edges of the petals just barely touch those of the top flower. Attach 4 more flowers at this level.

4. Wire down about 1", and trim the flower stems. Add another row of 5 flowers at this level. Continue in the same manner until all of the flowers have been used.

5. After wrapping the last row, lightly wrap the assembly wire down the stem for another 3 1/2". Wire all 4 leaves in place with their bases even.

6. Cut the leaf wires all at different lengths, and continue wrapping the assembly wire to the bottom of the stem.

7. Beginning tightly below the bottom row of flowers, use the remaining green beads to bead the stem. End 1" below the leaves. Tape over any visibly exposed assembly wire.

Dwarf Apple Blossom

Most deciduous fruit tree blooms are quite similar. However, ornamental varieties have much larger flowers. If you would rather have the larger flowers, simply double the amount of petal-color beads you need. Then make each petal a double row instead of a single.

Materials Needed

1 hank of white or pink beads (for petals)
1/2 hank of light green beads
2 strands of yellow beads
26-gauge beading wire
34-gauge gold beading wire
30-gauge assembly wire
Three 18" pieces of 16-gauge stem wires
1/2" green floral tape
1/2" brown floral tape

Flowers

Make (approximately) 60 (petal color)

a. Leaving at least 2" of bare wire at the beginning and end, make five 3/4" Continuous Loops.

b. Don't twist the wires.

Stamens

Make (approximately) 60

a. String the yellow beads onto the 34-gauge gold wire.

b. Leave 2" of bare wire at the beginning and end. Using one bead at a time, slide the bead into position, and twist it between your thumb and forefinger until you have about 1/4" of twisted wire.

c. Move another bead forward 5/16" from the first, and repeat the procedure. Be sure to twist the second bead until the bare wire between the first two stamens is used completely.

d. Repeat this procedure until you have 10 stamens in the group (fig. 37).

Figure 37

Leaves (pointed top, pointed bottom)
Make 8 (green)
1/2" basic, 7 rows

a. Reduce to 2 wires, and twist.

b. Tape the stems with 1/4" green tape.

Assembly

1. Use brown floral tape to lightly tape 1 stem wire. Set this aside.

2. Hold the other 2 stem wires tightly together, and wrap them with brown tape.

Flowers

1. Bring one of the cut end wires across the top of the flower and down between the first and second petals on the opposite side. This will close the flower.

2. Position a stamen group in the center of the flower. Bring the wires down the sides and under the bottom. Twist all 4 wires together. Leaving the bottom 3/4" bare, tape with 1/4" green tape. Repeat for all flowers.

Groups

1. Hold 5 flowers together with the bottoms of the floral-taped area even. Tightly wrap the bottoms of the taped area 2 or 3 times with assembly wire. Tape over this assembly area with brown tape.

2. In the same manner, make 4 groups of 2 leaves each.

Branches

1. Hold the first flower group so that the taped area extends beyond the tip of the thinnest stem wire. Use assembly wire to wrap it in place. DON'T cut the assembly wire. Wrap the wire down the branch at least 1", and add another flower group.

2. Wrap the wire down the branch at least 1", and add another flower group.

3. Wrap the wire down the branch at least 1", and add a leaf group.

4. Wrap the wire down the branch at least 1", and add another leaf group.

5. Wrap the wire down another 2" before cutting. Tape over the assembly area with brown tape, beginning at the tip and going down about 1 1/2" below the last leaf group.

6. Assemble the large branch in the same manner, using all the remaining flower and leaf groups. Drop down the stem about 2", and wire both stems together. Cut the bottom wires to the same length, and tape with brown tape.

Cyclamen

My book on houseplants claims that this is a favorite among blooming houseplants. Since mine is hanging over the edge of the pot, with its blooms lying on the table, I wonder if it isn't my favorite to buy and kill. Any shade of pink, red, or white can be used for this unusual plant.

Materials Needed

2/3 hank of petal-color beads

1 hank of green beads

1 to 3 strands of gray, white, or pale green beads

15 yellow beads

26-gauge beading wire

34-gauge gold wire

30-gauge assembly wire

Three 9" pieces of 20-gauge stem wire (for leaf stiffening)

16" of 16-gauge stem wire

1/2" green floral tape

Petals (pointed top, round bottom) (Lace all of the petals.)

Make 5 (petal color)

1 1/2" basic, 9 rows (Leave 3 wires, and twist.)

Stamens (yellow on 34-gauge wire)

Make 1

Use the same procedure as the Dwarf Apple Blossom stamen to create a 15-branched stamen group (See fig. 37, page 75).

Leaves (slightly pointed top, notched, round bottom) (Lace all of the leaves.)

Make 3 (green)

1/4" basic, 31 rows

    a. Begin by making your basic wire with 2 large basic loops. Do this by making the regular basic wire and loop with 1 full twist at the joint.

    b. Then form the second basic loop, and wrap the wire once around the basic wire.

    c. Use hemostats or pliers to help twist the basic loops for 1/4" to 1/2" (fig. 39). Hold a stiffening wire against the back (Stem Stiffening Method 1), and begin.

    d. Make rows 1 through 13 with a round top and round bottom.

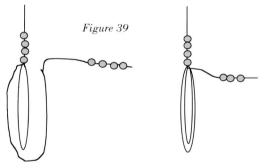

Figure 39

    e. After completing row 13, cut open the bottom of 1 of the basic loops, and spread the 2 ends slightly.

    f. For the rest of the leaf, wrap the bottom of each row around one of these cut wires, instead of the remaining basic loop (fig. 40). This will form a notch in the bottom of the leaf.

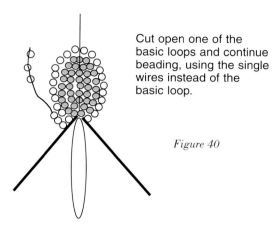

Cut open one of the basic loops and continue beading, using the single wires instead of the basic loop.

Figure 40

    g. As you work rows 14 through 25, add an extra bead to the top of the basic wire to create a slight point.

    h. After completing row 25, measure 3 feet of bare wire, and cut the petal from the spool.

    i. Shade the outside edge of the leaf by completing the next 2, 4, or all 6 of the remaining rows in gray, white, or pale green.

    j. When you are done beading, leave 5 feet of bare wire, and cut the wire from the spool.

    k. Weave the bare wire and the 2 cut, basic wires along the edges of the notch, and back up to the original basic loop. All stem wires should now be in the same place.

    l. Twist the stem wires together, and tape.

Assembly

1. Lightly tape the stem wire.

2. Position the stamen assembly against the tip of the stem, so that only 1/2 of the length of the stamens is above the stem. Wire this in place.

3. Add all 5 petals at once, with the edges overlapping. Wire these in place also, being very careful to wrap the assembly wire tightly against the bottom edge of the beads. Tape the stem.

4. Keeping in mind that you want the bend to occur in the beaded portion of the petal, not the bare wire, bend each petal down sharply. Give each petal a 1/4 twist in its center.

5. Bend the stem in the shape of a shepherd's hook, so that the stamens are pointed toward the ground.

6. Position the bloom and the leaves at attractive heights, and wire their bottoms together. Trim the stems, and tape over the assembly area.

Cactus

Beware! This little guy is as hard to handle as the live ones! My mother is the only person I know who prefers to grow her cactus from seed. I never shared her fascination with these little monsters. Now, as I bandage my fingers, I like them even less. Mom, this one is in your honor.

Materials Needed

1 hank of green beads
1/2 hank of orange beads
4" of yellow beads
26-gauge gold wire
26-gauge beading wire
30-gauge wire (for lacing and assembly)
1/2" green floral tape

Stamen-Pistil Group
Make 1 (green and yellow)
    a. String 4" of yellow beads, and add 1 1/2" of green beads. Leave 6" of bare wire.

    b. Make three 1/2" Continuous Loops of green. Pinch them together to form the pistil. Surround them with eight 1/2" Continuous Loops of yellow.

    d. Wrap the wire twice around the other wire, at the end closest to the loops.

    e. Measure 6" of bare wire, and cut. Don't twist.

Petals (round top, round bottom)
Make 1 (orange)
    a. Leave 2" of bare wire at the beginning and the end.

    b. Make nine 1" Continuous Loops.

    c. Lightly twist the wires.

Make 10
3/4" basic, 3 rows (Reduce to 1 wire.)
Make 12
1" basic, 3 rows (Reduce to 1 wire.)

Cactus (pointed top, pointed bottom)
Make 6 (green)
1" basic, 17 rows
    a. Leave 3 wires, and twist.

    b. DON'T trim the top basic wires.
Make 68
Cut sixty-eight 1 1/2" pieces of gold wire.

Assembly

Flower
1. Slip the long wires of the stamen-pistil group through the center of the orange Continuous Loops. Wrap twice with assembly wire.

2. Directly below, add the 10 small petals, and wire them in place.

3. Again, directly below, add the 12 large petals. Secure them with the assembly wire. DON'T trim the long pistil wires! They are needed to secure the flower later.

4. Twist all of the stem wires together tightly, and tape the twisted area.

5. Bead the top 1" of stem, and cover the assembly wire with tape.

Cactus
1. After lacing, fold all 6 pieces in half lengthwise, front sides inward to a 60° angle. Gather all the top basic wires together and twist tightly. Tuck the twisted wires down between 2 of the pieces.

2. To attach the thorns, begin at the very top of each of 5 of the combined petal edges. Use 2 cut wires at a time. Thread the wires through each of the outer rows of beads on two connecting pieces, center them, and give them one full twist. Continue along the petal edges, spacing the thorn groups about 1/2" apart. On the sixth edge, don't put a thorn group at the top. This will leave a small gap for the flower to be inserted.

3. Carefully slip the flower through the gap, and push it down until no tape is showing. Pull the long wires down through the bottom. Firmly twist them together with all the bottom wires. Trim the bottom, and tape.

4. Separate all the wires of the thorn groups, and trim them to 1/2" each.

Gardenia

My darling husband loves the scent of gardenias. Even though this one has no scent, he insisted that I make him one. I added scented oil to the pot. He loves it!

Materials Needed

1 hank of white beads

3 strands of medium green beads

1/2 hank of dark green beads

26-gauge beading wire

30-gauge assembly wire

One 18" piece of 16-gauge stem wire

1/2" green floral tape

Petals (round top, round bottom)
Make 2 (center petals) (white)
3-bead basic, 7 rows (Reduce to 1 wire.)
Make 6 (white)
5-bead basic, 9 rows (Reduce to 1 wire.)
Make 6 (white)
8-bead basic, 9 rows (Reduce to 1 wire.)
Make 6 (white)
12-bead basic, 11 rows (Reduce to 1 wire.)

Small Leaves with Sepals (pointed tops, round bottoms)
Make 3 (medium green)
8-bead basic, 7 rows, and 2 loops
a. After completing all 7 rows, add two 2" single loops to the base of each petal.

b. Pinch the loops closed. These will act as the sepals (see fig. 24, page 20).
c. Reduce to 2 wires, and twist.

Leaves (pointed tops, round bottoms)
Make 3 (dark green)
12-bead basic, 9 rows (Leave 3 wires, and twist.)
Make 3 (dark green)
16-bead basic, 11 rows (Leave 3 wires, and twist.)

Assembly

1. Lightly tape the stem wire.
2. Begin with the 2 center petals. Fold each sharply backwards, lengthwise. Hold them with the folds together to form a bud, and twist the wires.
3. Use assembly wire to attach the 6 small petals directly below, letting each petal slightly overlap the previous one. Bend the tips back, but leave the petals upright.
4. Add the 6 medium petals, and then add the 6 large petals in the same manner. Bend the tips back, but bend all of these down into a more "open" position.
5. Directly below the bloom, add the three leaf-sepal pieces. Position them so that a sepal is centered under each petal.

6. Drop down the stem 1", and add the 3 small leaves, all at the same level.
7. Drop down another inch, and add the 3 large leaves.
8. Tape over all exposed wires.

Note: If you use this as a shrub, add 1" and 2" 4-row Crossover Loops, twisted into spirals, as buds. Make both in medium green.

The plant on page 3 is constructed from 13 separate stems. Three are flowers, five are large buds, and five are small buds. Each stem has sepals and nine leaves.

Trillium

The perfect first flower for any beginner! In white or dark pink, this is just a beautiful little wildflower.

Materials Needed

4 strands of white or pink beads

8 strands of green beads

18 yellow beads

26-gauge beading wire

30- to 34-gauge assembly wire

12" of 16-gauge stem wire

1/2" green floral tape

Petals (pointed top, round bottom)

Make 3 (white or pink)

3/4" basic, 11 rows (Reduce to 2 wires.)

Sepals (pointed top, round bottom)

Make 3 (green)

1/2" basic, 9 rows (Reduce to 2 wires.)

Stamen

Make 1 (yellow)

a. Put all 18 yellow beads on the assembly wire. Leave 2" of bare wire.

b. Make 6 continuous 1/2" loops with only 3 beads on each.

c. Twist the loops, leave 2" of bare wire, and cut. Twist the wires.

d. Reduce to 2 wires.

Leaves (pointed top, round bottom)

Make 3 (green)

1/2" basic, 21 rows

a. Add an extra bead to the basic wire on each row, after row 10.

b. Reduce to 2 wires.

Assembly

1. Lightly tape the stem wire.

2. Center the stamen assembly among the 3 petals. Twist all the wires. Use assembly wire to attach this to the stem.

3. Position the sepals below and between the petals. Secure with wire and tape the assembly area. Drop down 2", wire, and tape all 3 leaves at the same level. Tape down the stem.

This slender lily will add a touch of drama to any bouquet. The natural colors are white, red, yellow, gold, orange, pink, and deep red. The plant has strap-like leaves, but they are usually gone by the time the blooms appear.

Although the flower grows in clusters, imagine how wonderful single blooms would look in a bouquet

Materials Needed

2 hanks of petal-color beads
2 strands of yellow beads
26-gauge beading wire
30- to 34-gauge assembly wire
Six 18" pieces of 16-gauge stem wires
1/2" green floral tape

Spider Lily

Petals (pointed tops, round bottoms)
(Lace all of the petals.)

Make 36 (petal color)
2" basic, 5 rows
    a. Leave 3 wires, and twist.
    b. When you have completed 3, twist the wires together (12 groups of 3 petals).

Stamens

Make 36 (yellow and petal color)
    a. Add 12 yellow beads to the wire that's holding the petal beads.
    b. Close to the tip, make two 6-bead loops.
    c. Twist well, and wrap the bare wire around the space between the loops.
    d. Measure 3" of the petal-color beads and 2" of bare wire. Then cut.
    e. Once you have completed 3 stamens, twist their wires together. Make 12 groups of 3 stamens.

Assembly

1. Lightly tape the 18" stem wires.
2. Use assembly wire to attach 2 stamen groups to a stem wire. Then attach 2 petal groups in the same manner. Tape over the assembly area.
3. Curl all of the petals back, and curl all of the stamens upwards. Assemble the other 5 flowers in the same manner.
4. If you are displaying the flowers in a cluster, group all of the stems together. Two inches from the blooms, wire the stems together, and tape.

Hypoestes

My oldest brother, Mike, is a landscaper who specializes in shrub propagation. I am dedicating this plant to him. It has NO flowers.

Materials Needed

1 1/2 hanks each of light green and white beads (mix evenly before stringing)
26-gauge beading wire
30- to 34-gauge assembly wire
18" of 16-gauge stem wire, cut in 3 pieces (5", 6", and 7")
1/2" green floral tape

Assembly

1. Lightly tape all 3 stems.

2. Use assembly wire to attach the leaves to the stems. Attach the smallest leaves on the tip. Attach the remaining leaves in order of size, using the list below.

3. Assemble 2 leaves at a time, on opposite sides. Turn 90°, drop down about 1/4", and attach the next 2 leaves. Tape over assembly wire. Join the three stems together, wire, and tape.

Leaves per stem:
Small Stem—4 small, 4 medium
Medium Stem—2 small, 2 medium, 6 large
Large stem—2 small, 2 medium, 2 large, 12 extra large

Leaves (pointed top, round bottom)
Make 8
1/2" basic, 7 rows (Leave 3 wires, and twist.)
Make 8
3/4" basic, 9 rows (Leave 3 wires, and twist.)
Make 8
1" basic, 11 rows (Leave 3 wires, and twist.)
Make 12
1" basic, 13 rows (Leave 3 wires, and twist.)

$\mathcal{S}$weet $\mathcal{V}$iolet

This little woodland favorite can be used to decorate almost anything. You can make it purple, pink, white, or yellow.

Materials Needed

4 strands of petal-color beads
4 strands of green beads
24 yellow beads
26-gauge beading wire
1/2" green floral tape

Flowers
Make 8 (petal color)

a. Leave 5" of bare wire. Using 1" of beads for the loops, make four 3-row Continuous Crossover Loops.

b. On the fifth loop, use 3/4" of beads for the inside loop, and make a Double Continuous Crossover Loop (5 rows).

c. Cut the wire to 6". Wrap the wire across the center of the flower to tighten the blossom.

d. Intending to form an "X" in the center of the flower, bring the wire back to the top between the first two petals made.

e. Add 3 yellow beads to the wire.

f. Pull the wire back down on the opposite side to complete the "X."

g. Pull the wires tight, and twist.

h. Tape the stem with 1/4" tape.

i. Repeat until you have completed all the flowers.

Leaves (pointed top, round bottom)
Make 3 (green)

1/2" basic, 21 rows (Leave 3 wires, and twist.)

$\mathcal{A}$ssembly

1. Twist all of the flower stems together.

2. Position the 3 leaves. Wire and tape them in place.

Crocus

In my hometown, these flowers are not only the first signs of spring, but they often have to pop their blooms up through the melting snow. What a welcome sight! These are usually found in white, yellow, blue, or purple, as well as variegated purple and white.

Materials Needed

1/2 hank of petal-color beads
1/2 hank of dark green beads
18 yellow beads
26-gauge beading wire
28-gauge gold wire (for the stamens)
30- to 34-gauge assembly wire
6" of 16-gauge stem wire
1/2" green floral tape

Petals (round top, pointed bottom)
   Make 6 (petal color)
   1/4" basic, 13 rows (Leave 3 wires, and twist.)

Stamens
   Make 1 (yellow)
   a. Put the beads on the gold wire.
   b. Position 3 beads 2" from the end of the wire. Hold the beads, and twist for 3/4".
   c. Position the next 3 beads 3/4" from the first, and twist.
   d. Continue until you have 6 stamens (see fig. 37, page 75). Leave 1" of bare wire, and cut.
   e. Bring the bottom wires together and twist.

Leaves (pointed top, pointed bottom)
   Make 6 (green)
   3" basic, 5 rows (Leave 3 wires, and twist.)

Assembly

1. Lightly tape the stem wire.

2. Use assembly wire to attach the stamen to the end of the wire.

3. Add 3 petals, and wire in place. Add the last 3 petals, and secure.

4. Cut all the secured wires at different lengths to taper. Tape over the construction area and down the stem.

5. Attach all 6 leaves at the same level, 2" down from the blooms.

6. Finish by taping over the construction area.

Shamrocks

I don't think Daddy has a favorite flower. However, since he came from Ireland to America as a young adult, we all supply him with a vast assortment of shamrocks. It's just a small thank you for being such a wonderful father.

Materials Needed

3 strands of green beads
3 strands of white beads
26-gauge green wire
1/2" green floral tape
(optional)

Leaves
Make 15
    a. Leave 4" of bare wire. Using 8 beads for the inner loop, make 3 Continuous Double Loops of beads.
    b. Leave 4" of bare wire, and cut from the spool.
    c. Twist the wires together.

Flowers
Make 8
    a. Leave 4 1/2" of bare wire. Make 8 Continuous Loops of 12 beads each.
    b. Leave 4 1/2" of bare wire, and cut.
    c. Pinch all of the loops closed. Pinch them into a tight bunch.
    d. Twist the wires together.

Assembly

Twist the bottom inch of each flower stem with the bottom inch of a leaf stem. If you choose, you may gather them all together, twist the bottoms, and tape them. Otherwise, they can simply be inserted as singles into a pot of moss-covered clay.

Projects with French-Beaded Flowers

Cymbidium Corsage

With this, you can wear flowers anytime you wish! It's a little too heavy for lightweight blouses, but looks great on most dresses and jackets.

Materials Needed

1 Cymbidium blossom
(DON'T trim the stem wires!)
Several violets or single-loop
flowers (optional)
8 feet of 2" petal-color, wire-edged, ribbon
8 feet of 1" contrasting-colored, wire edged, ribbon
Clear craft cement (Liquid Nails Clear®, or E6000®)

Assembly

1. If you're using small flowers also, position them around the cymbidium. Twist all of the wires together.

2. Cut the wires to a 3" length. Wrap them with floral tape.

3. Fan-fold the 1" ribbon at 5 1/2" intervals.

4. Mark the center, and poke a hole through all of the layers. Slide this over the flower stem. Repeat the same procedure with the 2" ribbon, folding it at 6" intervals.

5. Push both ribbons tightly against the flower(s). Place a small amount of glue around the stem to hold the flower(s) in place.

6. Once the glue dries, bend the stem at a 90° angle. Turn the corsage over to fluff and arrange the ribbon.

7. Use a hatpin or large safety pin to attach the corsage to your lapel.

Materials Needed

1 Rose (from pattern) or another flower
Several beaded leaves (of your choice)
28-gauge beading wire
Clear craft cement (Liquid Nails
    Clear, or E6000)
Krazy® Glue
1 metal hair barrette (found in the
    bead aisle of most craft stores)

Although this is a simple process with any flower, I just happened to have a rose handy.

 Assembly

1. Position your leaves and flower(s) along the barrette to check the fit. Add more if necessary to make sure that the beads will extend beyond the metal on all sides.

2. Place your flower upside down on the table. Place several drops of Krazy Glue on the twisted stem wires where they meet the petals. Set this aside to dry.

3. Open the barrette. Position a leaf (or group of leaves) so that the tips extend at least 1/4" beyond the end of the barrette. Make sure that no metal is showing. Cut a 2" piece of wire, and fold it in half. From the bottom, position the wire so one end goes through a hole in the end of the barrette and the other goes around the side. Push the wire through the leaf. Bring the wires together, and twist. Trim the wires to 1/8", and tuck them down between the rows of beads. Repeat this procedure on the other end of the barrette.

4. Bring the leaf stem wires (from both ends) to the center of the barrette, and twist them together. Trim the twisted wire to 1/4". Flatten it against the back of the barrette.

5. Using a scrap piece of wire, dab a small amount of the clear craft cement to the tip of each of the bent basic wires on the back of each of the flower and leaf petals. Make sure that the glue touches both the wire and the beads. This will keep the flower from becoming entangled in the wearer's hair.

6. Place a nice sized blob of clear cement on the center of the barrette. Make sure that it also covers the trimmed leaf wires. Turn the flower(s) over and carefully cut off the stem. Immediately, position the bloom on the cement-covered barrette.

7. Allow the glue to dry overnight. In the morning, if you find that you have too much cement, use nail clippers to remove the excess.

Shasta Daisy Napkin Ring

Although I chose the daisy, you can use this same method with different flowers to create a whole host of napkin rings to honor each particular season.

Materials Needed

4 strands of white beads
1 strand of yellow beads
3 strands of green beads
One 6" piece of paper-covered stem wire
26-gauge beading wire
30-gauge assembly wire
1/2" green floral tape

Petals

Make 2 (white)

a. Leaving 3" of bare wire at the beginning and end, make twelve 3-row Crossover Loops. Use 2" of beads for each main loop.

b. When completed, give the end wires a couple of twists.

Centers

Make 2 (yellow)

1-bead basic, 10 rows

a. Bend the basic wire and loop backwards after row 3 to create a raised button effect.

b. Since this has an even number of rows, you will end at the top. Leave 3" of wire, and cut it from the spool.

c. Cut open the basic loop at the bottom.

Sepals

Make 2 (green)

Leaving 2" of wire at the beginning and end, make six 3/4" Continuous Loops.

Assembly

1. Position the centerpiece over the petals. Bring the 4 wires down underneath to the center bottom. Push the wires up, flat against the bottom of the flower.

2. Twist the wires together with the end wires from the petal group.

3. Use assembly wire to attach the daisy to the end of the 6" stem (fig. 41).

Figure 41

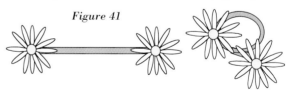

4. Place an upward bend in the center of each sepal loop. Place the sepals tight against the bottom of the petals. Twist the end wires together. Use assembly wire to secure them in place.

5. Follow the same procedure to attach the second daisy to the other end of the same stem wire.

6. Use the rest of the green beads to bead the entire stem, from daisy to daisy. To end, wrap the wire several times, directly below the bottom daisy, and cut. Put 1 drop of Krazy Glue on the tip of the cut wire.

7. Using a wire spool as a guide, gently bend the stem into a circle until the flowers overlap.

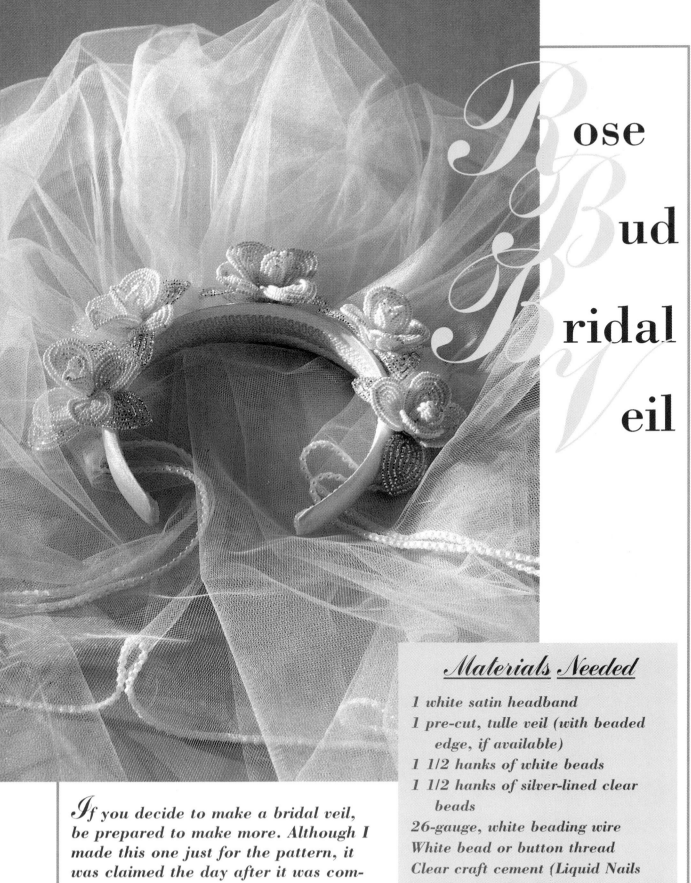

Rose Bud Bridal Veil

If you decide to make a bridal veil, be prepared to make more. Although I made this one just for the pattern, it was claimed the day after it was completed. What a simple and elegant way to add love to the bride's trousseau.

Materials Needed

1 white satin headband

1 pre-cut, tulle veil (with beaded edge, if available)

1 1/2 hanks of white beads

1 1/2 hanks of silver-lined clear beads

26-gauge, white beading wire

White bead or button thread

Clear craft cement (Liquid Nails Clear, or E6000)

Krazy Glue

Petals (round top, round bottom)
  Make 10 (white)
  4-bead basic, 7 rows (Reduce to 1 wire.)
  Make 20 (white)
  4-bead basic, 11 rows (Reduce to 1 wire.)

Leaves (pointed top, round bottom)
  Make 15 (silver)
  12-bead basic, 9 rows (Reduce to 1 wire.)

Assembly

Flower

1. To form the bud, fold 2 small petals in half lengthwise. Make sure that the petal backs are facing inward. Interlock the folds, and twist the 2 wires lightly.

2. Hold 2 petals, opposite each other, directly below the bud. Add 2 more petals at right angles to the first 2. Twist all of the wires together, just until firm.

3. Form a triangle of 3 leaves tight against the flower, and tightly twist all of the wires.

4. Turn the bloom upside down, and add 2 or 3 drops of Krazy Glue to the twisted stem wires where they meet the flower. Set aside to dry.

5. Cut the twisted flower stem to 1/2". Dip the entire 1/2" stem in clear craft glue, and allow it to dry overnight. Complete the other 4 flowers in the same manner.

Veil

1. Wash your hands thoroughly before beginning.

2. Measure 3" up from the tip of each leg of the headband. Make a small pencil mark on the top back edge. Measure the distance between the marks, and divide it by 4. This is the distance between flowers. Measure each one and make a small pencil mark. You now should have 5 marks and 5 flowers.

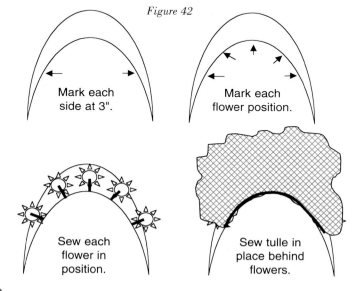

Figure 42

Mark each side at 3".

Mark each flower position.

Sew each flower in position.

Sew tulle in place behind flowers.

3. Align the end of a coated flower stem with the back top edge of the headband. Make sure to hold it on a pencil mark, and sew it securely in place. Add each flower in the same manner (fig. 42).

4. Gently lay the tulle over the rose buds (right side down). Match the sewing edge of the veil to the top, back edge of the headband. Adjust it so that the side edges extend 1" past each of the lower flowers.

5. Carefully sew the tulle to the headband, as close to the flowers as possible. Make all of the stitches small, tight, and even. Pull the tulle back over the sewn area, and fluff.

Index

Watch for new patterns on my Web site!
http://www.beadedflowerpatterns.com

Some of my favorite Web sites:
Download Patterns, Instantly – www.bead-patterns.com
Beads – www.shipwreck.com
Artistic® Wire and Colored Floral Tape – www.judyheller.com
Bulk Craft Wire – www.cbcmetal.com
Bead Spinners – www.beadspinnerlady.com
Other Information – www.beadworkbycaren.com

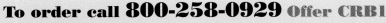